FULL-FRONTAL

FULL-FRONTAL
Male Nudity Video Guide

S T E V E   S T E W A R T

COMPANION PRESS

Laguna Hills, California

Copyright © 1996 by Steve Stewart

COMPANION PRESS
PO Box 2575, Laguna Hills, California 92654

Printed in the United States of America
First Printing 1996

ISBN: 0-9625277-7-7

To Jim—for everything.

CONTENTS

ACKNOWLEDGMENTS

Over the years I've put together nearly a dozen video guides. The thing I enjoy most about the process is that it's a true collaboration involving many people.

Once again, I'm grateful to the dozens of individuals who have provided assistance—the studios and mail-order houses who have sent me complimentary screener videos; previous readers who have alerted me to videos; friends who have kept a lookout for videos; and photographers who have donated photos, just to name a few.

For their generosity in providing photos and screeners, I would like to especially thank Tom Hopkinson at Award Films International/Insider Video Club and David Mortimer and Matthew Moore at Alluvial—Greenwood/Cooper. Also helpful were Mike Stimler at Water Bearer Films and Marcus Hu at Strand Releasing. Charles Moniz and Roy Windham at Baby Jane in West Hollywood also provided assistance in obtaining hard-to-find and rare photos from their terrific collection of celebrity nudes.

Many thanks too, to Valerie Frazee who has brought a keen eye to bear on the editing and proofing of this guide and has been helpful in countless other ways. I'm also grateful to Lance Perkins for his production help.

Over the years many movie buffs have contributed in ways both large and small as well. They include: Bill Daniels, Steve Desjardins, Gillian Flynn, Boze Hadleigh, Troy Hatlevig, Marcus Hu, Dave Hutchinson, Jamoo, Don Lort, James Robert Parish, Georgene Rada, Benjamin Russeau, Bette Siegel, Peggy Stuart, Brenda Sunoo and Vin Tozzi.

I would also like to thank Aaron Silverman at SCB Distributors for his helpful suggestions and vital support of this guide.

Last, but definitely not least, I would like to thank my partner, Jim Fredrickson, for his constant support, advice and encouragement. I couldn't have done it without him.

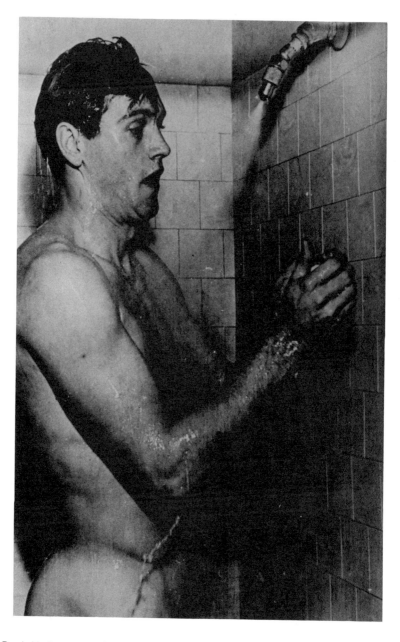

Rock Hudson never had an on-screen full-frontal nude scene, but like so many popular actors, before and after him, he was captured off-screen in the buff, if only in this teaser.

INTRODUCTION

"Male nudity distracts the audience."
—*Michael Caine,*
Entertainment Tonight

Okay, I admit it. I'm a video voyeur. Even worse, I'm a video voyeur with a mission. When you watch 365-plus videos a year, as I do, (Okay, I'm also a bit obsessive) you don't miss much. Other than real life, that is.

WHY THIS BOOK WAS WRITTEN

After watching the first few thousand videos, I began to notice that it's easier to find an actor drinking his own urine (even Kevin Costner did it in *Waterworld*) than exposing his genitals on video. Something Kevin Costner never has done. Somewhere along the line it occurred to me that I might be able to provide a valuable service (value being relative) by saving other less-obsessive video voyeurs the time and effort. So, I began cataloging these rare occurrences in this video guide. Besides making me feel like the Mother Theresa of male nudity, it also helps me justify being such a couch potato.

WHO THIS GUIDE IS WRITTEN FOR

This book isn't written for the Michael Caines of this world. Or for certain unnamed, all-powerful video mega stores. Or for former right wing Presidential candidates. It's written for curious movie buffs who don't mind seeing their favorite stars in the buff. It's also written for individuals and audience members who don't mind being "distracted."

THIS GUIDE IS INTENDED
TO SAVE YOU TIME

It's not that there aren't video guides to male nudity already on the market. I've just found them, for the most part, difficult to use and not exactly comprehensive. Having to wade through hundreds of videos featuring celebrity buns is often like looking for a needle in a haystack, so to speak. It's not that there's a lack of full-frontal male nudity on video, it's just not easy to find.

Having to look through a telephone book-sized guide is also not my idea of handy. So I narrowed the focus of my guide simply to full-frontal male nudity. If you want to find male butts, I recommend the other guides.

HOW TO USE THIS GUIDE

To keep it simple, I've divided this guide into four sections: Main-

Getting his start as a nude model, Joe Dallesandro became famous in Andy Warhol's underground movies for his full-frontal nude scenes. He later went on to do legitimate mainstream movies like *The Cotton Club* (1984).

stream Videos, Foreign Videos, Naturist/Nudist Videos and Special-Interest Videos. All listings in each section are referenced by film title from A to Z. An index at the back of the guide will help you search by actor, director or title.

RENTER AND BUYER BEWARE

Do you remember William Baldwin's full-frontal nude scene in *Sliver*? How about Sylvester Stallone's full-frontal nude scene in *Demolition Man*? What about Bruce Willis' willie in *Color Of Night*?

No? Well that's because they never made it to American screens intact. This, despite abundant press and promotion by publicists and members of the Loraina Bobbit fan club, hyping each actor's privates for months prior to their respective film's release. Teasing audiences with the possibility of seeing their favorite stars full-frontal has become a very common and deceptive practice.

When renting or purchasing a video, always look for the NC-17 version, unrated version or director's cut. Most videos are edited before they reach the video store. Some are edited to include extra nudity that wasn't included in the theatrical release (director's cut); others to remove nudity (usually R versions of an NC-17 rated film). This also applies to foreign films. I've heard from film buffs in other countries that videos distributed there usually contain much more full-frontal nudity than the same videos released in this country.

YOUR COMMENTS ARE WELCOME

If you happen to be even more obsessive than I am and know of a video I've left out, please let me know and I'll include it in the next edition of this guide and give you credit in the acknowledgments. A guide like this is nothing, if not a collaboration. Send your comments, criticisms or suggestions to PO Box 2575, Laguna Hills, CA 92654 or e-mail me at Qcompanion@aol.com.

I look forward to hearing from you.

Steve Stewart
Laguna Hills, 1996

MAINSTREAM
VIDEOS

MAINSTREAM VIDEOS

This one falls under the heading "They don't come any bigger than this!" In its March 1992 issue, *Spy* magazine printed this rare picture taken of Hollywood's biggest box-office superstar, Arnold Schwarzenegger, in his early body-building days.

ABDUCTORS, THE   1971
Richard Smedley
A full-frontal shower scene.

ABOUT LAST NIGHT   1986
Rob Lowe
An extremely brief, partial frontal scene in kitchen.

ALL THE RIGHT MOVES   1983
Tom Cruise
A very brief frontal nude scene taking off clothes in bedroom before having sex with his girlfriend.

ALMOST PREGNANT   1991
Steve Adell
A brief, frontal nude fantasy scene.

AMERICAN FLYERS   1985
David Grant
A very brief frontal shot of actor setting on his bed while undressing for a shower.

AMERICAN GIGOLO   1979
Richard Gere
Difficult to see full-frontal scene standing near a window.

AMERICAN TABOO   1984
Jay Horenstein
A brief, difficult to see full-frontal shower scene.

AMERICAN WEREWOLF
IN LONDON, AN   1981
David Naughton
Several frontal shots throughout film.

ARIA   1987
James Mathers
A full-frontal nude bathtub scene.

ARMED FOR ACTION   1992
Rocky Patterson
A very brief, partial frontal nude bathroom scene.

ASPEN EXTREME   1993
Peter Berg
A brief frontal shot of Berg at night on a snowy road. Difficult to see much.

AT PLAY IN THE FIELDS OF
THE LORD   1991
Tom Berenger
Difficult to see full-frontal shot as he strips in front of a group of natives.
Niilo Kivirinta
Extensive full-frontal nude scenes, running and playing in the forest with

Tom Berenger, pictured here in *At Play In The Fields Of The Lord* (1991), is another big-name actor who is no stranger to frontal nudity in the movies. He also did full-frontal nudity in his first film, *In Praise Of Older Women* (1977).

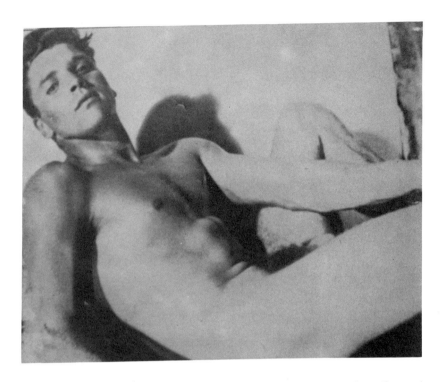

The late Burt Lancaster is another of Hollywood's biggest stars from the past who posed nude off screen. He is pictured here in the early days before he became an actor.

other nude native children.

AUDITIONS 1978
Corey Brandon, Rick Cassidy, Rick Lutz, William Margold and Harry Osborn
A full-frontal nude scene during an audition for a skin flick.

BABYMAKER, THE 1970
Scott Glenn
Brief full-frontal scene.

BACKFIRE 1987
Jeff Fahey
A full-frontal nude shower scene.

BAD COMPANY 1994
Fred Henderson
A brief full-frontal nude scene.

BAD LIEUTENANT, THE 1992
Harvey Keitel
A full-frontal drunken nude scene.

BASIC INSTINCT 1992
Bill Cable
A brief full-frontal nude scene playing a corpse in bed.

BASKET CASE 1981
Kevin Van Hentenryck
A full-frontal dream sequence of young

Recognize this press-shy superstar? This is reported to be an early photo of Warren Beatty, and he certainly has no reason to be shy.

man running down the street.

BEACH GIRLS, THE 1982
James Daughton
A very brief full-frontal nude skinny dipping scene.

BEAUTIFUL DREAMERS 1991
Rip Torn
A brief frontal skinnydipping scene.

BEEN DOWN SO LONG IT LOOKS LIKE UP 1971
Barry Primus
A full-frontal nude scene.

BENEATH THE VALLEY OF THE ULTRAVIXENS 1979
Ken Kerr
A full-frontal nude shot in this sexploitation film.
Steve Tracy
A full-frontal scene of actor about to be seduced by an older woman.

BEYOND INNOCENCE 1988
Unidentified
Full-frontal nudity of a group of young men in a lockerroom.

BEYOND LOVE AND EVIL 1969
Marc Coutant
A full-frontal shot during a group ritual whipping.
Michel Lablais
Extended full-frontal nude scene.

BLACK MAGIC MANSION 1992
Paul Birchard
A dimly-lit, full-frontal shot in the shower.

BLONDY 1976
Matthieu Carriere
A full-frontal nude scene during sex.

BLOODY MAMA 1970
Clint Kibrough
A full-frontal bathing scene.

BLUE LAGOON, THE 1980
Christopher Atkins
Brief full-frontal shot underwater and coming down a waterfall.
Glenn Kohan
A full-frontal nude scene of the actor playing the young Christopher Atkins.

BLUE VELVET 1986
Kyle Mac Lachlan
A brief full-frontal scene while running to hide in a closet.

BODY MELT 1993
Unidentified
A full-frontal nude scene during sex.

BODY OF EVIDENCE 1992
Willem Dafoe
Brief, full-frontal nude sex scenes with Madonna.

BODY OF INFLUENCE 1993
Nick Cassavetes
A very brief, full-frontal nude sex scene.

BORN ON THE FOURTH OF JULY 1989
Unidentified
A full-frontal nude scene of patient being bathed.

BOXING HELENA 1993
Bill Paxton
A very brief full-frontal scene sitting in bed.

BOYS OF CELLBLOCK Q, THE 1993
Andrew Adams, Lewis Alante,
Danny Parr, Damian Perkins,

Michael Valdes
A full-frontal nude shower scene.

BOYS' SHORTS 1992
Unidentified
A brief, full-frontal nude shot and numerous shots from behind.

BRAINWASH 1982
Walter Olkewicz
A full-frontal nude scene after being forced to strip.

BRAVEHEART 1995
Unidentified Group
A group of soldiers, including Mel Gibson, raise their kilts to flash the enemy in a full-frontal long shot. Difficult to see anything.

BREATHLESS 1983
Richard Gere
Frontal shower scene.

BRIDGES TO NOWHERE 1985
Stephen Judd
A full-frontal skinnydipping scene.

BRITANNIA HOSPITAL 1982
Malcolm McDowell
An extended full-frontal scene on operating table. Looks like a possible prop.

BUSTER AND BILLIE 1974
Jan-Michael Vincent
An extensive full-frontal nude skinny-dipping scene.

Pictured below in *The Blue Lagoon* (1980), Christopher Atkins is one of many actors who got his start in a film that required him to do full-frontal nudity. He tried it again in *A Night In Heaven* (1983), but since only has done nudity in movies from behind.

One of the few Hollywood actors who is proud of his body,
Christopher Atkins appeared naked through most of his first
mainstream film, *The Blue Lagoon*.

CAGED TERROR 1971
Percy Harkness
A full-frontal nude bedroom scene.

CALENDAR GIRL 1993
Jason Priestley
A very brief, frontal nude scene while walking on a nude beach.

CALIGULA 1979
Donato Placido
A full-frontal nude sex scene.
Malcolm McDowell
A full-frontal scene dancing outside in the rain.
Unidentified
Full-frontal shots of a variety of nude men throughout the film.

CAROLINE AT MIDNIGHT 1993
Clayton Rohner
An extremely brief, full-frontal nude scene getting into a bathtub.

CARRIED AWAY 1996
Dennis Hopper
A full-frontal nude scene.

CASTAWAY 1986
Oliver Reed
A full-frontal nude scene on a deserted island.

CAT CHASER 1988
Tony Boland
A full-frontal nude scene as actor is forced to strip.

Like the photo of Warren Beatty, this is reported to be an early candid of James Caan. The resemblance is un"caan"y.

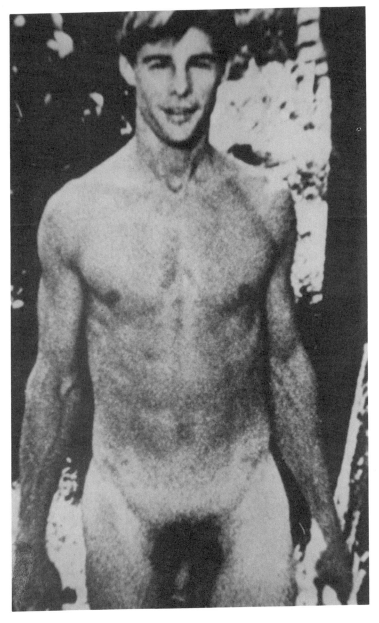

The first well-known actor to do an extensive full-frontal nude scene in a mainstream American movie was Jan-Michael Vincent. In the 1974 film *Buster and Billie*, he goes skinnydipping with his girlfriend.

A young and well-endowed Robby Benson appeared nude in a very dimly-lit shower scene in *Running Brave* (1983).

Thomas Milian
A full-frontal scene while undressing.

CAT PEOPLE 1982
John Heard
Partial frontal nude bathroom scene.

CENTERFOLD GIRLS 1974
Dennis Olivieri
A full-frontal scene.

CHAIN OF DESIRE 1993
Dewey Weber
Very brief, frontal nude shot getting out of a bath.

CHATTAHOOCHEE 1990
Gary Goldman
A very brief, difficult to see full-frontal nude scene during a strip search.

**CHEECH & CHONG'S
NICE DREAMS** 1981
Tommy Chong
A very brief, difficult to see full-frontal nude bedroom scene.

CIAO, MANHATTAN 1972
Allen Ginsberg
Full-frontal scene during a party.

CLEO/LEO 1989
Kevin Thomsen
A brief, full-frontal nude sex scene.

CLOCKWORK ORANGE, A 1971
Malcolm McDowell
A full-frontal scene during sex with two women, shot from a distance in fast motion. Again, stripping when he's taken into custody.

CLOSE MY EYES 1991
Clive Owen
A full-frontal sex scene.

COBB 1994
Michael Moss
A brief, frontal nude scene.

COLOR OF NIGHT 1994
Bruce Willis
A clear, but brief, partial frontal underwater nude scene.

COMING OUT UNDER FIRE 1994
Unidentified
Full-frontal male nudity in film clips and stills.

CONTRACT, THE 1972
Bruno Pradal
A violent full-frontal nude scene.

CONVICT'S WOMEN 1972
Harvey Cross
Full-frontal nude scenes throughout the film.

COVERGIRL 1982
Jeff Conaway
Brief frontal shot getting out of bed.

CRIMINAL PASSION 1993
John Allen Nelson
Extended full-frontal nude scene in a swimming pool.

CRY UNCLE 1971
Allen Garfield
A brief, partial frontal nude scene.

CRYING GAME, THE 1992
Jaye Davidson
A full-frontal nude scene exposing his character in drag to be a man.

**CURSE OF THE STARVING
CLASS** 1994
James Woods
An outdoors frontal long shot while

stripping off his clothing in the rain.

DANGEROUS TOUCH 1993
Lou Diamond Phillips
A difficult to see full-frontal nude scene behind a shower curtain.

DANTON 1982
Unidentified
A full-frontal nude modeling scene.

DEER HUNTER, THE 1978
Robert DeNiro
Brief frontal nudity outdoors.

DEMOLITION MAN 1993
Sylvester Stallone
European versions reportedly include a

full-frontal scene edited to a butt shot in the United States.

DESPERATE REMEDIES 1994
Kevin Smith
A full-frontal scene while bathing.

DIGITAL MAN 1995
Don Swayze
A very brief, partial frontal nude bedroom scene.

DINAH EAST 1970
Reid Smith
A full-frontal scene losing his towel.

DON'T LOOK NOW 1973
Donald Sutherland

Malcolm McDowell appears in several full-frontal nude scenes in the futuristic *A Clockwork Orange* (1971). Here he and his teenaged friends wear cock-shaped codpieces as symbols of their virility as they terrorize the locals.

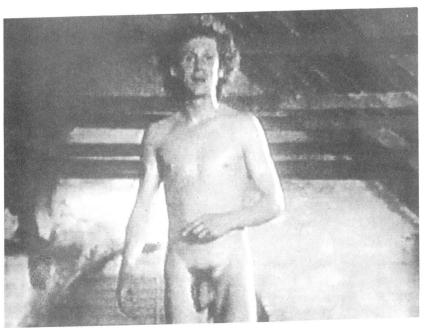

A young and very uninhibited Peter Firth has numerous lengthy full-frontal nude scenes throughout *Equus* (1977).

A brief full-frontal scene while dressing.

DREAMS COME TRUE   1985
Michael Sanville
Numerous full-frontal sex scenes.

DRIVE, HE SAID   1971
Michael Margotta
An extensive full-frontal nude scene.

ECHOES   1983
Dickson Lane
Extended full-frontal nude art modeling scene.

EMMANUELLE, JOYS OF A WOMAN   1975
Frederic Lagache
Partially obscured full-frontal bathing scene.

EMMANUELLE'S REVENGE   1986
Unidentified
A full-frontal nude sex scene.

ENDANGERED   1994
Kent MacLachlan
A very brief full-frontal skinnydipping scene.

ENFORCER, THE   1976
Unidentified
A full-frontal nude sex scene.

EVIL LAUGH   1986
Myles O'Brian
A very brief, full-frontal bedroom scene.

EQUUS   1977
Peter Firth
Several extensive full-frontal scenes throughout the film, both outdoors and indoors.

FANNY HILL   1983
Unidentified
Full-frontal shots of a variety of nude men throughout the film.

FAST WALKING   1981
M. Emmet Walsh
A full-frontal nude scene after sex.

FEAR HAS A THOUSAND EYES   1973
Hans Wahlgren
A full-frontal nude scene.

FEAR NO EVIL   1981
Daniel Eden
A full-frontal scene in the school showerroom.

FEMALE TROUBLE   1974
Michael Potter
Several full-frontal nude scenes.

FINGERS   1978
Harvey Keitel
A brief frontal nude scene.

FIRST CIRCLE, THE   1972
Peter Steen
A full-frontal nude, prison strip-search scene.

FIRST NUDIE MUSICAL, THE   1975
Alan Abelew
Full-frontal nude scene while dancing on stage.

FISHER KING, THE   1991
Robin Williams
A dimly-lit, difficult to see frontal nude scene of him dancing in a park at night.

FLESH   1968
Joe Dallesandro
Extensive full-frontal nude scenes

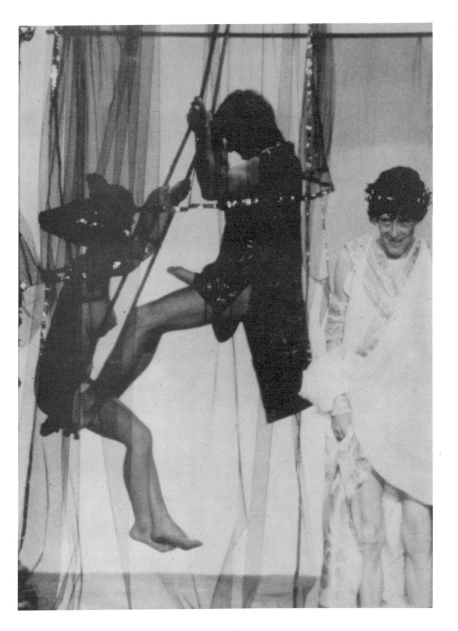

Pictured above is one of many full-frontal nude scenes featured in the x-rated version of the controversial mainstream movie *Caligula* (1979).

Like Arnold Schwarzenegger, Ed Fury (pictured above and right) got his acting start in the 1950s as a bodybuilder. Unlike Arnold, he never made it beyond B-movies.

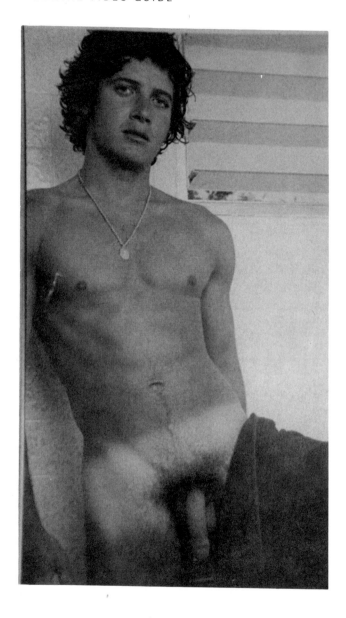

Soap opera actor Steve Bond showed off his considerable talents in this photo for *Playgirl* magazine. He went on to do feature roles in films like *H.O.T.S.*, but his on-screen parts have never been as big as his off-screen parts.

Willem Dafoe appeared in a long shot full-frontal scene hanging from a cross in *The Last Temptation of Christ* (1988).

throughout the film.

FLESH GORDON 1974
Jason Williams
A brief, full-frontal nude scene before he dresses in drag. Most of the male cast is also featured in full-frontal nude scenes.

FORTRESS 1992
Unidentified
Brief full-frontal shot of group of men entering prison.

FORTUNE AND MEN'S EYES 1971
Michael Greer
A full-frontal nude scene after performing in drag. He takes off outfit and stands naked before the audience.

FRANKENSTEIN
Randy Quaid 1994
Full-frontal scene of Quaid as the naked monster comes to life.

FRIEND OF THE FAMILY 1995
Michael Jay
Underwater frontal shot. Very difficult to see anything.

FUN DOWN THERE 1990
Michael Waite
A full-frontal nude scene of him lying in bed.

GAME OF SEDUCTION 1976
John Finch
A full-frontal nude sex scene.

GHOST STORY 1981
Craig Wasson
A violent full-frontal nude scene.

GINGER 1970
Calvin Culver
Extensive full-frontal bedroom scene.

Don Johnson, Bruno Kirby and Gregory Harrison all had full-frontal nude scenes in *The Harrad Experiment* (1973), a classic, 1960s-era free-love extravaganza.

GLEN AND RANDA   1971
Steven Curry
Several blurry, full-frontal nude scenes outdoors in the woods.

GLITTER DOME, THE   1984
Neal Andrews
A full-frontal nude scene of a man acting in a porn movie.

GOODBYE, EMMANUELLE   1977
Jean-Pierre Bouvier
A full-frontal nude scene of him having sex on the beach.
Umberto Orsini
A very brief, full-frontal nude scene while putting on clothes.

**GREAT ROCK 'N' ROLL
    SWINDLE**   1979
Paul Cook, Steve Jones
Full-frontal scene running on the beach.

GRIEF   1993
Alexis Arquette
A very brief, partial frontal nude gay sex scene.

HARDCORE   1979
Tim Dial
Brief, partial frontal nude scene while auditioning for a porn film.
Gary Rand Graham
A dimly-lit, full-frontal nude scene acting in a porn film.

HARRAD EXPERIMENT, THE 1973
Michael Greene
A full-frontal group scene.
Gregory Harrison
Numerous full-frontal scenes.
Don Johnson
A brief frontal nude scene drying off after a shower.
Bruno Kirby

Malcolm MacDowell has appeared nude in the movies more than any other mainstream actor. Here he dances in the rain in *Caligula* (1979), one of the most sexually-explicit films of the decade.

Hollywood hunk Brad Pitt has bared his butt many times on screen, but full-frontally only off-screen.

A brief frontal skinnydipping scene.
Elliott Street
A full-frontal skinnydipping scene.

HARVEST, THE   1992
Miguel Ferrer
Very brief frontal nude scene getting out of bed.

HAUNTED SUMMER   1988
Eric Stoltz
Lengthy full-frontal skinnydipping scene.

HERO AIN'T NOTHIN'
BUT A SANDWICH, A   1977
Larry B. Scott
Full-frontal scene of boy being bathed.

HIRED HAND, THE   1971
Robert Pratt
A very brief, full-frontal skinnydipping scene.

HITCHHIKERS, THE   1971
Norman Klar
A full-frontal skinnydipping scene.

HOLLYWOOD HOT TUBS   1984
Mark Costello
A full-frontal nude, gay bathhouse scene.

H.O.T.S.   1979
Steve Bond
Brief full-frontal nude scene.

HOW TO SUCCEED WITH SEX 1970
Zack Taylor
Full-frontal nude scenes.

HUSBANDS AND LOVERS   1992
Julian Sands
Lengthy full-frontal shower and sex scenes.

I LIKE TO PLAY GAMES   1994
Ken Steadman
A brief full-frontal nude scene in bedroom.

IF YOU DON'T STOP ...
YOU'LL GO BLIND!   1987
Rod Hasse
A full-frontal medium shot sex scene on stage.

IMAGINE: JOHN LENNON   1988
John Lennon
A full-frontal image of album cover.

IN PRAISE OF OLDER
WOMEN   1977
Tom Berenger
Very brief full-frontal nude scenes during sex.

IN THE HOUSE OF SPIRITS   1993
Josh Maguire
A full-frontal skinnydipping scene.

INDIAN RUNNER, THE   1991
Viggo Mortensen
An extended full-frontal bedroom scene looking into a full-length mirror.

INSERTS   1975
Stephen Davies
Extended full-frontal nude scenes throughout the film.

INSIDE OUT   1992
Joseph Malone
A long shot, partial frontal nude scene.
Scott Mitchell
A very brief frontal sex scene.

ITALIAN STALLION, THE   1970
(a.k.a. A Party At Kitty and Stud's)
Sylvester Stallone
A number of full-frontal nude scenes.

Chris Mulkey has two lengthy full-frontal nude scenes in the independent drama, *Patti Rocks* (1988). In this night scene, he flashes passing cars from the side of the road.

JERKER 1991
Joseph Stachura
A full-frontal nude sex scene.

JOSEPH ANDREWS 1977
Peter Firth
A frontal scene while being stripped of his clothes.

JULIA HAS TWO LOVERS 1990
David Duchovny
Very dark silhouette of frontal nudity while standing at window. Difficult to see anything.

JUNGLE HOLOCAUST 1985
Massimo Foschi
Full-frontal scene while being tortured.

KEEP IT UP 1971
Michael Stearns
Full-frontal sex scenes.

KILLING HOUR, THE 1982
David Ramsey
A full-frontal scene as a corpse.
Unidentified
A full-frontal nude modeling scene.

LADY CHATTERLY'S LOVER 1981
Nicholas Clay
A full-frontal nude scene while bathing.

LAST EMPEROR, THE 1987
Unidentified
A full-frontal nude scene of young emperor being bathed.

LAST PICTURE SHOW, THE 1971
Gary Brockette, Randy Quaid
A full-frontal scene of two men getting out of a pool after skinnydipping.

LAST RITES 1988
Robert Corbo
A dimly-lit, full-frontal bedroom scene.

**LAST TEMPTATION
    OF CHRIST, THE** 1989
Willem Dafoe
Very brief long shot of actor on cross. Difficult to see anything.

LETTERS FROM VIETNAM 1987
Unidentified

Full-frontal nude skinnydipping scene.

LIGHT OF DAY 1987
Billy Sullivan
A full-frontal scene of child bathing.

LITTLE DARLINGS 1980
Unidentified
A full-frontal long shot of a group of boys skinnydipping in a lake.

LITTLE DRUMMER GIRL, THE 1984
Moti Shirin
A full-frontal nude scene in prison.

LONG LIVE THE KING 1977
Freeman King

Tony Goldwyn has numerous nude scenes in *Love Matters* (1993), including a brief and dimly-lit full-frontal scene while having sex in a kitchen.

A full-frontal showerroom scene.

LOOKING FOR LANGSTON 1992
Unidentified
Full-frontal nude stills.

LORDS OF DISCIPLINE 1983
Unidentified
A full-frontal nude shower scene involving one of the young cadets.

LOSIN' IT 1982
Unidentified
A full-frontal nude shower scene featuring a group of boys.

LOVE BITES 1988
Christopher Ladd
Extensive full-frontal nude shower scene.
Erich Lange
A full-frontal sex scene.
Tom Wagner
A full-frontal nude, gay sex scene.

LOVE CIRCLES AROUND THE WORLD 1984
Timothy Wood
A full-frontal nude, sex scene.

LOVELESS 1981
Willem Dafoe
A dimly-lit, full-frontal nude, sex scene.

LOVE MATTERS 1993
Tony Goldwyn
A very brief, frontal nude scene.

LOVE ME DEADLY 1972
L. William Quinn
A full-frontal sex scene.

LUCIFER RISING 1967
Bobby Beausoleil

A full-frontal nude scene of actor playing the devil.

MAGIC GARDEN OF STANLEY SWEETHEART, THE 1970
Don Johnson
A brief, full-frontal nude scene on stage.

MALA NOCHE 1987
Tim Streeter
A dimly-lit, full-frontal scene in Gus Van Sant's first feature.

MAN CALLED HORSE, A 1970
Richard Harris
Several very brief frontal nude shots outdoors.

MANDINGO 1975
Perry King
An extended full-frontal bedroom scene.

MARRIED PEOPLE, SINGLE SEX 1993
Bob Rudd
A brief frontal shot in the shower.

MARTIN'S DAY 1985
Martin Buckert
A difficult to see full-frontal long shot of actor skinnydipping.

MARY SHELLEY'S FRANKENSTEIN 1994
Robert DeNiro
A brief, obscured frontal shot playing the monster coming to life.

MASTER BEATER, THE 1968
John Lee
A full-frontal gay sex scene in softcore film.

Actor Sam Jones got his start posing nude for *Playgirl* magazine in June 1975. He went on to roles in *"10"* (1979), *Flash Gordon* (1980) and *My Chauffeur* (1986). In the latter, he ran through a park buck naked, but the only exposure is from the rear.

Like many rock stars before him, Sting parlayed his musical talents into a movie career. And, like many other actors, his full-frontal nudity has been strictly off-screen.

MEDIUM COOL 1969
Robert Forester
A full-frontal sex scene.

MINX, THE 1968
Tim Lewis
A brief, full-frontal sex scene.

MIXED COMPANY 1974
Unidentified
Full-frontal shots of a variety of nude men in the shower.

MODERNS, THE 1988
Unidentified
A full-frontal nude scene of a man walking down the street.

MURDER AMONG US: THE SIMON WIESENTHAL STORY 1989
Ben Kingsley
A brief, frontal nude scene while in a concentration camp.

MURDER IN THE FIRST 1994
Kevin Bacon
A brief, dimly-lit full-frontal silhouette in jail scene.

NAILS 1992
Dennis Hopper
A very brief frontal scene after dropping his towel.

NAKED APE, THE 1973
Johnny Crawford
A dimly-lit, frontal shot of actor portraying a human specimen in a museum exhibit.

NAKED IN NEW YORK 1994
Eric Stoltz
A lengthy full-frontal scene while standing naked on the beach during a dream sequence.

NAKED INSTINCT: BEYOND THE SEXUAL LIMIT 1993
Len Di Stafano
Full-frontal while masturbating.
Greg Fawcett
Frontal shot while taking a bath with a woman.
David Poole
Frontal nudity during a sex scene.
Peter Stoddard
A full-frontal scene during hot tub sex scene.
Hutch Williams
A full-frontal nude scene while performing for a female officer.

NAME OF THE ROSE, THE 1986
Christian Slater
Partial frontal scene while making love.

NEMESIS 1992
Tom Janes
Brief frontal shots during sex scenes.

NEVER CRY WOLF 1983
Charlie Martin Smith
Brief, full-frontal skinnydipping scene.

NEW AGE, THE 1994
Unidentified Group
An extended full-frontal nude scene of man at swingers' party.

NEW YEARS DAY 1989
David Duchovny
The well-endowed *X Files* TV star appears in a frontal shower scene.

NIGHT CLUB 1989
Nicholas Hoppe
A full-frontal nude scene.

NIGHT IN HEAVEN, A 1983
Christopher Atkins
Brief full-frontal while pulling down

his pants during sex scene.

NIGHT OF THE DEMON 1979
Rob Camp
A brief frontal shot while peeing in the woods.

NIGHT PORTER 1973
Nino Bignamini
A full-frontal nude scene of a man getting out of bed. Contains other incidental frontal male nudity as well.

NO SKIN OFF MY ASS 1993
Bruce La Bruce
Numerous full-frontal sex scenes.
Klaus Von Brucker
Numerous full-frontal sex scenes.

NOMADS 1985
Pierce Brosnan
Dimly-lit, full-frontal nude scene of him walking to bed.

NOSTRADAMUS 1993
Anthony Higgins
A brief, full-frontal bathroom scene.
Tcheky Karyo
A long shot full-frontal nude scene.

NOW AND THEN 1995
Devon Sawa
A brief frontal shot of the boy as his towel flies open while bending down to pick up his underwear. The scene takes place outdoors during the day.

OH! CALCUTTA! 1980
Mark Dempsey, Bill Macy, Mitchell McGuire, Gary Rethmeier
Extended full-frontal nude scene during this filmed version of the stage play.

ONE NIGHT STAND 1984
Jay Hackett

A long shot full-frontal strip poker scene.

OUT COLD 1989
Tom Byrd
Extremely brief, full-frontal nude scene of the actor getting out of bed.

OUTING, THE 1987
Mark Mitchell
A full-frontal nude scene.

PARADISE 1981
Willie Aames
Brief, dimly-lit, partial frontal nude shot of actor standing in the ocean near the shore.

PATTI ROCKS 1987
Chris Mulkey
One lengthy full-frontal scene in a public restroom. A second scene with the character having his underwear pulled down in public.

PEOPLE NEXT DOOR, THE 1970
Sandy Alexander
A full-frontal nude scene of the actor getting out of bed.

PEREZ FAMILY, THE 1995
Lazaro Perez
Extremely brief, full-frontal nude scene after jumping out of a tree. Nude from behind for most of the film.

PERFECT TIMING 1984
Paul Boretski
A full-frontal nude scene during sex.

PERSONAL BEST 1982
Kenny Moore
An extensive full-frontal nude scene of the actor getting out of bed and walking into the bathroom to pee.

GEORGE MAHARIS

George Maharis is an actor best known for his TV series *Route 66*. He also appeared in a handful of films, including *The Satan Bug* (1964), but he made an even bigger impression when he posed nude for *Playgirl* magazine. Like so many others, he unfortunately kept his clothes on in his films.

Sylvester Stallone got his start in porn films like *A Party At Kitty and Studs,* which features much full-frontal nudity. This publicity still from the movie *Demolition Man* (1993) appeared in the Italian magazine *Babilonia.* As is often the case, frontal nudity was deleted from the American version of the film.

PICKUP, THE 1975
Alan Long
Extended full-frontal nude scene.

PIECES 1983
Ian Serra
A dimly-lit, full-frontal bedroom scene.

PINK FLAMINGOS 1972
Danny Mills
A full-frontal, bestiality sex scene.

PINK MOTEL 1982
John Macchia
A very brief, full-frontal nude bedroom scene.

PLAYER, THE 1992
Tim Robbins
A brief, obscured, full-frontal nude scene of the actor covered with mud.

PLAY TIME 1994
Craig Stepp
Several brief, partial frontal nude scenes.
David Elliott
Several full-frontal nude scenes.

**PLEASURE DOING
    BUSINESS, A** 1978
Richard Karron
A very brief, partial frontal nude scene.

POISON 1991
James Lyons
A full-frontal, gay sex scene.

POLICEWOMAN 1974
Phil Hoover
A full-frontal shower scene.

POPI 1969
Miguel Alejandro
Extensive full-frontal nudity.

POSSE 1993
Charles Lane
A very brief, frontal nude scene.

**POSSESSION OF
    JOEL DELANEY, THE** 1972
David Elliott
A full-frontal scene of a young boy forced by an older man to strip.

PREDATOR II 1990
Corey Rand
A full-frontal scene of the actor hanging upside down while being tortured.

PROJECT: METALBEAST 1994
John Marzilli
Actor appears in full-frontal shot as a dead werewolf.

PULP FICTION 1994
Bruce Willis
A very brief, partial nude scene in shower.

QUIET EARTH, THE 1985
Bruno Lawrence
A difficult to see, outdoor, full-frontal nude scene.

RANCHO DELUXE 1975
Jeff Bridges
A brief, full-frontal long shot scene of the actor running, outdoors.

RAPTURE, THE 1991
David Duchovny
Brief frontal nudity of actor getting out of bed.

RECKLESS 1984
Aidan Quinn
A full-frontal long shot in high school shower and later in very brief sex scene.

RED SHOE DIARIES: GIRL ON A BIKE   1995
Brent Fraser
A very brief, full-frontal nude sex scene.

REINCARNATION OF PETER PROUD, THE   1975
Tony Stephano
Appears in several brief, frontal nude scenes throughout the film.

RETURN OF THE SECAUCUS 7   1980
Bruce McDonald, David Strathairn
A full-frontal skinnydipping scene.

REVENGE OF THE CHEERLEADERS   1976
David Hasselhoff
A brief frontal shower scene.

ROB ROY   1995
Liam Neeson
An extremely brief, dimly-lit frontal shot of actor coming out of a lake after bathing.

ROOM WITH A VIEW, A   1985
Julian Sands
A memorable and lengthy, full-frontal, skinnydipping scene involving other men as well.

Joe Dallesandro is one of those rare actors who became famous because of his full-frontal nude scenes in a number of '60s and '70s Andy Warhol cult films. He later parlayed his exposure into a legitimate acting career. He is pictured above and right in publicity stills from *Heat* (1972), in which he did not have a frontal nude scene.

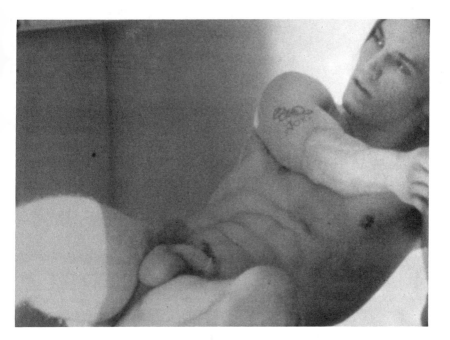

Joe Dallesandro is another actor not ashamed of his body. At a recent autograph session, he signed photos of himself for hundreds of his eager fans.

RUNNING BRAVE   1983
Robby Benson
A full-frontal nude shower scene. Very difficult to see anything in dim light.
Francis Danburger
A full-frontal nude scene snapping towels in the boys locker room.
Jeff McCracken
Full-frontal nude scene in locker room.

SAINT JACK   1979
Edward Tan
A full-frontal nude sex scene with actor playing a male hustler.

SATISFACTION GUARANTEED 1973
Michael B. Abbott
Full-frontal nude scene.

SCANDAL   1989
Unidentified
A group of men appear in full-frontal nude scene during an orgy.

SCHINDLER'S LIST   1993
Unidentified
Casual full-frontal scenes involving men and women in a concentration camp.

SCORE   1973
Calvin Culver
Extensive full-frontal scenes.
Gerald Grant
A very brief, full-frontal nude bedroom scene.
Carl Parker

A lengthy full-frontal nude sex scene.

SECRET GAMES 3   1994
Woody Brown
A brief frontal shot when underwear is pulled down.
Unidentified
A full-frontal nude scene involving two male customers having sex with prostitutes.

**SECRET OF ROAN
     INISH, THE**   1995
Gillian Byrne
Young lost boy appears in numerous frontal nude scenes running around naked on a deserted island.

SENSATION   1988
Blake Bahner
Extremely brief, lower frontal nude scene as character gets out of bed.

SHADOWZONE   1989
Robbie Rives
Several full-frontal nude scenes.

SHAMING, THE   1979
John Lafayette
A very brief, full-frontal scene as actor takes off his clothes.

SHELTERING SKY, THE   1990
John Malkovich
Brief full-frontal shot while getting out of hotel bed.

SHE'S GOTTA HAVE IT   1987
John Canada Terrell
A very brief frontal scene getting into bed.

SHORT CUTS   1993
Huey Lewis
A difficult to see, long shot full-frontal

of him peeing off a cliff.

SIESTA   1987
Gabriel Byrne
A brief, full-frontal long shot, of actor getting out of bed.

SINGLE WHITE FEMALE   1992
Steven Weber
A very brief frontal scene as the character gets out of bed after sex.

**SIX DEGREES OF
     SEPARATION**   1994
Lou Millione
An extended full-frontal nude scene of actor running around the living room.

SLAUGHTER HIGH   1985
Simon Scuddamore
A lengthy, full-frontal public nude scene.

SLEEPAWAY CAMP   1983
Unidentified
A full-frontal nude scene of young boy.

SLIVER   1992
Unidentified
Brief frontal nudity of a man being spied on through a surveillance camera.

SLUGS   1987
Kris Mann
A brief full-frontal scene as the actor runs from monster.

SMOKE   1993
Mark D'Auria
Several full-frontal nude scenes.

SOME GIRLS   1988
Patrick Dempsey
Extended frontal nudity while sitting on bed.

Tony Stephano appears in a publicity still for *The Reincarnation Of Peter Proud* (1975).

Aidan Quinn takes a shower in a deserted high school locker room in *Reckless* (1984). Later in the film (right) he is caught without his pants.

Andre Gregory
A brief, full-frontal scene near the end of the film, while sitting at his desk working in the nude.

SQUEEZE, THE 1977
Stacy Keach
Full-frontal nude stripping scene.

STARS AND BARS 1988
Daniel Day-Lewis
A full-frontal scene as the actor runs from hoods.

STATE OF SIEGE 1973
Unidentified
A full-frontal nude prison scene.

STATUE, THE 1970
Marco Gobbi

A full-frontal nude scene of actor running around on stage.

STEALING HEAVEN 1988
Derek De Lint
A brief, full-frontal nude scene while making love.

STEPFATHER, THE 1987
Terry O'Quinn
A brief, full-frontal shower scene.

STEPPENWOLF 1974
Pierre Clementi
Very brief, full-frontal nude sex scene.

STORMY MONDAY 1988
Sean Bean
A full-frontal nude scene while getting dressed.

STRANGER BY NIGHT 1994
Steven Bauer
A frontal nude scene during sex.

STREAMERS 1982
Matthew Modine
A full-frontal nude shower scene mostly obscured by steam.

STREET WARRIORS 1987
Angel Fernandez Franco
A full-frontal scene while being stripped.

STRIKE A POSE 1993
Robert Eastwick
A brief, partial frontal nude sex scene.

SUMMER LOVERS 1982
Peter Gallagher
Full-frontal long shot of the actor diving off a cliff into the ocean. Diffi-

cult to see much.

SUNSET GRILL 1992
Jerry Spicer
Very brief frontal as he is being thrown out of a room.

SUPER 8-1/2 1994
Klaus Von Bruker
Numerous full-frontal sex scenes.
Bruce La Bruce
Numerous full-frontal sex scenes.
(Strand)

SUPERGRASS, THE 1985
Adrian Edmondson
A brief, full-frontal scene of the actor taking off clothes.

SUPERMAN 1978
Aaron Smolinski
Playing the young Superman, he arrives

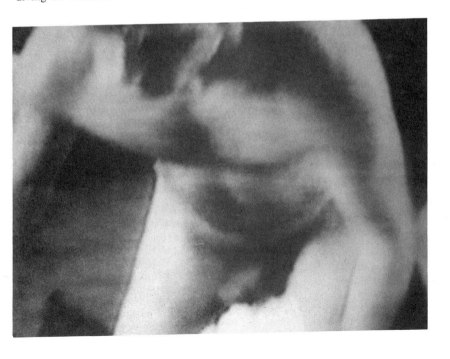

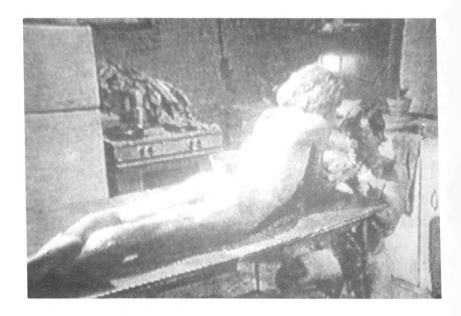

A very well-endowed Barry Tubb has several full-frontal nude scenes in *Warm Summer Rain* (1989). Here he crouches down on his knees and nearly drags the ground in this sex scene with Kelly Lynch, who also has a full-frontal scene.

in a spaceship au natural.

SUPERSTAR: THE LIFE AND TIMES OF ANDY WARHOL   1990
Candy Darling
A full-frontal still photo.

SWING SHIFT   1984
Ed Harris
Extremely brief, partial frontal of actor sitting down wearing only a towel.

TARZAN THE APE MAN   1981
Richard Harris
A full-frontal skinnydipping scene.

10 TO MIDNIGHT   1983
Gene Davis
Extensive full-frontal nude scene.

TERMINATOR, THE   1984
Arnold Schwarzenegger
Extremely brief, partial frontal nude opening scene.

TONGUES UNTIED   1989
Unidentified
A brief, full-frontal nude scene of actors on stage.

TOTALLY F***ED UP   1993
Unidentified
A full-frontal nude porno film scene. (Strand)

TRACKS   1976
Dennis Hopper
An extended full-frontal scene of actor on a train.

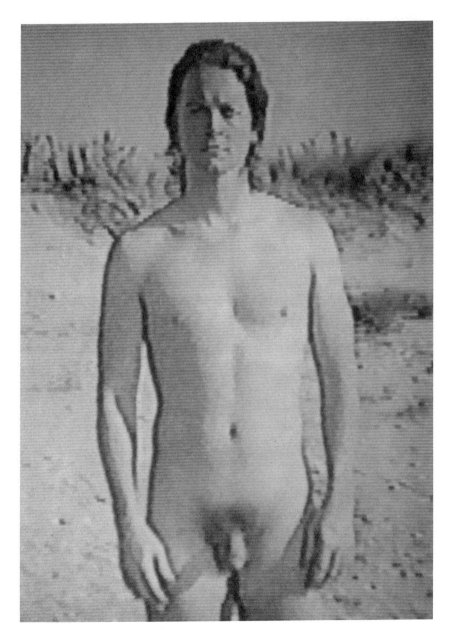

Eric Stoltz stands naked on a deserted beach in a lengthy dream sequence in the aptly named *Naked In New York* (1994).

In perhaps the most famous full-frontal nude scene in movie history, Alan Bates and Oliver Reed have a lengthy nude wrestling match in front of a fireplace in *Women In Love* (1969).

TRADE-OFF 1994
Adam Baldwin
A very brief, partial frontal nude bathtub scene.

TRASH 1970
Joe Dallesandro
Several lengthy full-frontal nude scenes.

**UNBEARABLE LIGHTNESS OF
    BEING, THE** 1988
Unidentified
Juliette Binoche looks at photos taken at a nudist colony depicting male and female full-frontal nudity.

UNDER SUSPICION 1992
Stephen Moore
A very brief, full-frontal, gay sex scene.
Unidentified
A full-frontal nude sex scene involving two men.

UNDER THE VOLCANO 1984
Albert Finney
A very brief, frontal scene of actor getting dressed.

VALENTINO RETURNS 1988
Barry Tubb
Dimly-lit, blurry, frontal skinnydipping scene.

VERY NATURAL THING, A 1974
Kurt Gareth, Robert Joel, Bo White
Full-frontal scenes on the beach and a full-frontal skinnydipping scene.

VIDEO VIXENS 1973
George "Buck" Flower
Full-frontal nudity while getting undressed.
Bernie Scorpio, Lennie Scorpio

A full-frontal nude scene of twins standing next to each other.

**WARLOCK 2: THE
    ARMAGEDDON** 1993
Julian Sands
Obscured frontal shot as another monster is born.

WARM SUMMER RAIN 1989
Barry Tubb
Extensive full-frontal nude scenes.

WEEDS 1987
Mark Rolston
A full-frontal scene of actor on stage.

**WHAT DO YOU SAY TO A
    NAKED LADY?** 1969
Norman Manzon
A full-frontal nude modeling scene.

WIGSTOCK—THE MOVIE 1995
Flloyd
A drag queen does a striptease before a large outdoor crowd to reveal he is a man. An extended full-frontal shot.

WOLFEN 1981
Max M. Brown
A brief, frontal nude scene of actor lying dead on a table.
Edward James Olmos
A very brief, full-frontal nude scene while being chased.

WOMEN IN LOVE 1969
Alan Bates, Oliver Reed
Extensive full-frontal nude scene while wrestling together.

WORKING GIRLS 1986
Roger Babb
A brief, full-frontal nude shot of actor during a sex scene.

WRITE TO KILL 1990
Scott Valentine
A very brief, partial frontal scene of actor getting into bed.

YOUNG LADY CHATTERLY 1977
Ray Martin
A full-frontal sex scene.

FOREIGN
VIDEOS

FOREIGN VIDEOS

ACLA 1992
(a.k.a. Acla's Descent
   Into Floristella)
Francesco Cusimano
A full-frontal nude scene of a young
boy. (Italy/Subtitles) (IVC)

ADVOCATE, THE 1994
David Larkin
Extended full-frontal shots during a
dream sequence featuring the actor
running around outdoors at night.
(UK)

**ADVENTURES OF A
   PRIVATE EYE, THE** 1974
Robin Stewart
A full-frontal, skinnydipping scene. (UK)

ALVIN PURPLE 1974
Graeme Blundell
A few very brief, full-frontal nude
scenes. (Australia)

Pier Paolo Pasolini's *Arabian Nights* (1974) features extensive male and
female frontal nudity. And like all of his films, it is a Pandora's box of sexual
fantasies.

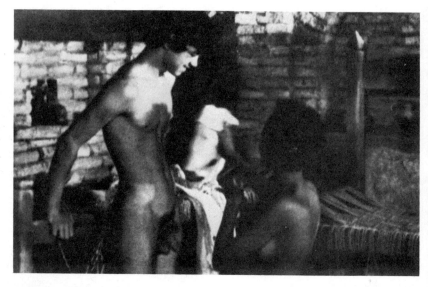

Another of many full-frontal nude scenes from director Pier Paolo Pasolini's *Arabian Nights* (1974).

ANDREA   1975
Jean-Marc Dupuich
A full-frontal nude scene while bathing.
Jacques Zolty
A full-frontal nude scene.
(France/Subtitles)

ANNUNCIATION, THE   1984
Bocsor Peter
A full-frontal nude scene of actor playing Adam, as a boy, in the garden of Eden. (Hungary/Subtitles)
(IVC)

ARABIAN NIGHTS   1974
Ninetto Davoli
Extended full-frontal nude scenes.
Unidentified
Full-frontal shots of a variety of nude men throughout the film.
(Italy/Subtitles) (IVC)

AUNTIE
(a.k.a Keep It Up, Jack) 1975
Mark Jones
A full-frontal nude scene in the shower.
(UK)

BEETHOVEN'S NEPHEW   1986
Dietmar Prinz
A full-frontal scene of the actor running down a hall. (UK)

BEST WAY, THE   1978
Patrick Deware
Extended full-frontal nude shot while undressing in bedroom. (France/ Subtitles)

BETTY BLUE   1986
Jean-Hughes Anglade
A number of full-frontal nude scenes.
(France/Subtitles)

The term full-frontal doesn't quite do justice to this unidentified actor in Pier Paolo Pasolini's *Canterbury Tales* (1971).

Above and right, in these behind-the-scenes photos from *The Decameron* (1970), Pier Paolo Pasolini directs a typical sex scene featuring the trademark male full-frontal nudity his films are known for.

BLONDE AMBITION 1980
R. Bolla, Eric Edwards
A full-frontal nude, hardcore sex scene.
(UK)

BODY MELT 1993
Robert Simper
A full-frontal nude scene. (Australia)

BOYS OF ST. VINCENT 1992
Unidentified
An extended scene of nude boys in a
shower room from behind and a brief
full-frontal shot of one boy. (Canada)
(IVC)

CANTERBURY TALES, THE 1971
Tom Baker
A full-frontal nude scene while getting
dressed.
Dan Thomas
A violent, full-frontal nude scene.
Unidentified

Includes many full-frontal shots of
unidentified actors.
(Italy/Subtitles) (IVC)

CAUGHT LOOKING 1991
Grant Cottrell
A full-frontal nude scene of actor play-
ing a sailor in fantasy sequence.
Donlagh O'Leary
A full-frontal nude modeling scene.
(UK) (Water Bearer)

CEMENT GARDEN, THE 1992
Andrew Robertson
A brief, full-frontal nude scene as he
walks into bedroom. (France/ Subtitles)

CHRONICLE OF A BOY
    ALONE 1964
Diego Puente
A group of boys appear in several full-
frontal nude scenes. (Argentina/ Subtitles) (IVC)

Director Paul de Lussanet's *Dear Boys* (1980) features extensive full-frontal
nude scenes of nearly all the male cast members, young and old.

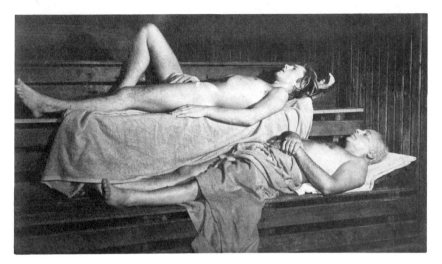

Actor Helmut Berger (above) only teases in *Dorian Gray* (1970) but has done full-frontal scenes both on and off-screen.

CLINIC, THE 1982
Danny Nash
An extended full-frontal while being examined. (Australia)

COLEGAS 1982
Jose Luis Fernandez Eguia
A full-frontal scene in the bedroom.
Antonio B. Pineiro
A full-frontal nude locker room scene. Includes other male nudity as well. (Spain/Subtitles) (IVC)

CONVERSATION PIECE, THE 1976
Helmut Berger
A frontal shower scene. (Germany/ Subtitles)

COOK, THE THIEF, HIS WIFE AND HER LOVER, THE 1990
Alan Howard
Extensive full-frontal nude scene. Film also contains other frontal male nude scenes. (UK)

DAMAGE 1992
Jeremy Irons
An extended full-frontal nude scene of actor running down a staircase. (UK)

DEAR BOYS 1980
(a.k.a Lieve Jongens)
Hugo Metsers
Extensive full-frontal nude, gay sex scenes of Metsers and most of the rest of the male cast.
(Denmark/Subtitles)

DECLINE OF THE AMERICAN EMPIRE, THE 1986
Remy Girard
A full-frontal nude scene as he gets out of bed after sex. (Canada/Subtitles)

DEVIL IN THE FLESH 1986
Federico Pitzalis
A lengthy full-frontal sex scene. (Spain/Subtitles)

DON JUAN, MY LOVE   1991
Juan Luis Gallardo
Several brief, full-frontal nude outdoor scenes. (Spain/Subtitles)

DON'S PARTY   1976
Graham Kennedy, Ray Barrett, John Hargreaves, Harold Hopkins
Full-frontal nude scene and skinny-dipping at the party. (Australia)

DRIFTING   1983
Unidentified
A full-frontal nude, gay sex scene. (Israel)

DROWNING BY NUMBERS   1988
Trevor Cooper
A full-frontal nude bedroom scene.

David Morrissey
A frontal scene in a swimming pool. (UK)

DULCES NAVAJAS   1981
Jose Luis Manzano
A lengthy, full-frontal nude scene. (Spain/Subtitles)
(IVC)

EAST OF ELEPHANT ROCK   1976
John Hurt
A full-frontal scene while getting dressed. (UK)

EDWARD II   1991
Dudley Sutton
A full-frontal scene of actor stripping down. (UK)

Nearly all of Spanish director Eloy De La Iglesia's movies feature extensive full-frontal male nudity. Pictured below and right is a scene from *El Diputado* (1979).

EL DIPUTADO 1978
Angel Pardo
A full-frontal nude sex scene. (Spain/Subtitles) (IVC)

EL SACERDOTE 1979
(The Priest)
Jose Franco
A lengthy, full-frontal, self-mutilation scene. Film features many other unidentified male frontal nude scenes as well. (Spain/Subtitles) (IVC)

EL TOPO 1970
Brontis Jodorowsky
Extensive full-frontal shots of boy throughout the film. (Mexico/Subtitles)

END OF THE GAME 1976
Jon Voight
Several brief, frontal nude scenes. (France/Subtitles)

EUROPA EUROPA 1991
Marco Hofschneider
Several lengthy, full-frontal nude scenes throughout the film. (Germany/Subtitles)

FATAL BOND 1991
Jerome Ehlers
Brief frontal nude scene of actor getting out of bed. (Australia)

FLAVIA, THE REBEL NUN 1974
Anthony Corlan
A full-frontal scene during sex. (Spain/Subtitles)

FLIRTING 1994
Unidentified
A full-frontal nude scene in the boys' shower room. Also features many of the boys nude from behind. (Australia)

Marco Hofschneider has extensive full-frontal exposure in the classic German film *Europa Europa* (1992). In this scene, he flees the Nazis and hides in a barrel.

FOR A LOST SOLDIER 1992
Unidentified
After a swim in the ocean, a teenaged boy named Jan lies naked on his stomach on the shore. When he rolls over, he is briefly exposed frontally. (Netherlands/Subtitles) (IVC)

FORBIDDEN PASSION 1985
Nick Reding
A casual, full-frontal nude scene of actor playing a hustler. (UK)

FOURTH MAN, THE 1984
Thom Hoffman
A long shot full-frontal scene.
Jeroen Krabbe
Several full-frontal nude scenes. (Netherlands/Subtitles)

FOX AND HIS FRIENDS 1975
Rainer Werner Fassbinder
Extensive full-frontal, bathhouse, nude scenes of Fassbinder and other male actors. (Germany/Subtitles)

FREEDOM IS PARADISE 1989
Volodya Kozyrev
A full-frontal nude, public shower scene. (Russia/Subtitles) (IVC)

FRIENDS FOREVER 1986
Morten Stig Christensen
A casual, full-frontal nude scene.
Thomas Sigsgaard
A casual, full-frontal nude scene. (Denmark/Subtitles)
(IVC)

HIDE AWAY 1991
Kasper Andersen, Allan Winther
A lengthy, full-frontal nude bathroom and shower scene.
(Denmark/Subtitles)
(IVC)

HOUSE OF ANGELS 1992
Unidentified
A lengthy, full-frontal nude, skinny-dipping scene involving a group of men and women. (Sweden/Subtitles)

HUSSY 1980
John Shea
A brief, partial-frontal nude sex scene. (UK)

I AM CURIOUS YELLOW 1967
Vilgot Sjoman
A full-frontal sex scene. (Sweden/Subtitles)

I AM MY OWN WOMAN 1992
Unidentified
A full-frontal nude scene while dressed in drag. (Germany/Subtitles)

I LOVE YOU
(a.k.a Eu Te Amo) 1982
Paulo Cesar Perelo
A brief, full-frontal nude bedroom scene. (Spain/Subtitles)

IN A GLASS CAGE 1986
Unidentified
Full-frontal nude stills at beginning of film. (Spain/Subtitles)

INHERITORS, THE 1984
Nikolas Vogel
A brief, frontal nude sex scene. (Germany/Subtitles)

JAMON JAMON 1992
Javier Bardem
A dimly-lit, full-frontal nude scene of a man pretending to be a bullfighter with a buddy in the moonlight.
Thomas Penco
A dimly-lit, full-frontal nude bullfight scene. (Spain/Subtitles)

The 1986 gay favorite, *Friends Forever,* features Henrik Ohlers (above and right) in an extensive full-frontal nude scene.

JEAN COCTEAU: AUTOBIOGRAPHY OF AN UNKNOWN   1983
Raymond Radiguey
A full-frontal nude still of Cocteau's lover. (France/Subtitles)

JESUS OF MONTREAL   1989
Lothaire Bluteau
A dimly-lit, partial-frontal nude scene while being crucified during an outdoor play. (Canada/Subtitles)

JOCK PETERSON   1974
Jack Thompson
Several full-frontal nude scenes. (Australia)

JUBILEE   1977
Unidentified
Full-frontal shots of a variety of nude young men throughout the film.

Ian Charleson
A full-frontal nude scene following a gay sex scene. (UK)

KANGAROO   1987
Colin Friels
A full-frontal long shot while skinny-dipping in the ocean.
Unidentified
Full-frontal shots of a variety of nude men at an Army induction center. (Australia)

KITCHEN TOTO, THE   1987
Edwin Mahinda
A full-frontal scene of a boy being bathed. (UK)

L' HOMME BLESSE   1988
(a.k.a. The Wounded Man)
Jean-Hughes Anglade

A brief, frontal nude scene.
Vittorio Mezzogiorno
A full-frontal nude scene. (France/Subtitles)

LABYRINTH OF PASSION 1982
Imanol Arias
A full-frontal nude scene partially obscured by subtitles. (Spain/Subtitles)

LAKKI: THE BOY WHO GREW WINGS 1992
Unidentified
A full-frontal nude scene of a well-endowed man walking down a hallway. (Norway/Subtitles) (IVC)

LAST OF ENGLAND, THE 1987
Spenser Leigh
A very brief, full-frontal gay sex scene. (UK)

LAW OF DESIRE 1987
Eusebio Poncela
A full-frontal nude bedroom scene. (Spain/Subtitles)

LESSONS AT THE END OF SPRING 1989
Danya Tolkachev
A full-frontal nude scene of a young boy in a public shower with other boys and men. (Russia/Subtitles). (IVC)

LIKE WATER FOR CHOCOLATE 1993
Marco Leonardi
An extended full-frontal shot after dying in bed. (Mexico/Subtitles)

LITTLE THIEF, THE 1989
Simon de la Brosse
A very brief, full-frontal nude scene getting into bed. (France/Subtitles)

Lino Brocka's *Macho Dancer* (1988) features male erotic dancers who strip on stage.

LONDON KILLS ME   1991
Steven Mackintosh
A full-frontal bathtub scene. (UK)

LORD OF THE FLIES   1963
Unidentified
Full-frontal shots of a number of nude boys throughout the film. (UK)

LOVERS   1992
Jorge Sanz
Lengthy full-frontal sex scenes. (Spain/Subtitles)

MACHO DANCER   1988
Unidentified
Brief full-frontal scene of a group of young men on stage. (Philippines/ Subtitles)

MAN BITES DOG   1992
Benoit Poelvoorde
Several full-frontal nude scenes. (France/Subtitles)

MAN IN UNIFORM, A   1994
Tom McCamus
A full-frontal nude scene of actor walking across the room. (Canada)

MAN LIKE EVA, A   1985
Werner Stocker
A dimly-lit, full-frontal nude shower scene. (Germany/Subtitles)

MAN OF FLOWERS   1983
Norman Kaye
Extended full-frontal nude scene of actor standing in bathroom. (Australia)

MAN WHO FELL TO EARTH, THE   1976
David Bowie
A partial-frontal nude sex scene. (UK)

MAP OF THE HUMAN HEART 1992
Robert Joamie
Full-frontal shot of a young boy being bathed. (Canada)

MARRIAGE OF MARIA BRAUN, THE   1979
George Byrd
A brief, full-frontal nude sex scene. (Germany/Subtitles)

MAURICE   1987
Rupert Graves
A lengthy full-frontal scene of actor getting out of bed after sex with James Wilby.
James Wilby
A full-frontal nude shot, of actor sitting in bed after a gay sex scene. (UK)

MAY WINE   1991
Unidentified
A full-frontal nude scene of the actor exposing himself to a woman. (France/ Subtitles)

MONTENEGRO   1981
Svetozar Cvetkovic
A full-frontal shower scene. (Hungary/ Subtitles)

MONTY PYTHON'S LIFE OF BRIAN   1979
Jackie Chan
A full-frontal nude scene of actor standing at the window. (UK)

MURMUR OF THE HEART   1971
Benoit Ferreux
A full-frontal scene of a young boy standing in a public shower. (France/ Subtitles)

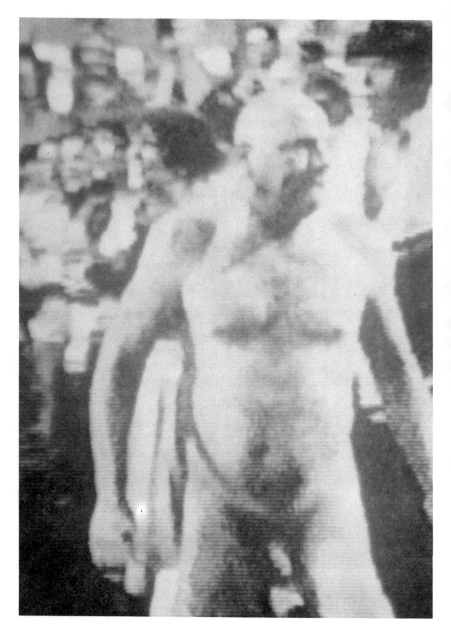

Several male characters are featured in extensive full-frontal scenes in both
Porky's (1981) and *Porky's II* (1983) (above).

Dan Monahan (above) plays Pee Wee and is featured in an extensive full-frontal nude scene in a cemetery at night in *Porky's II* (1983)

MY FATHER'S GLORY 1991
Julien Ciamaca
A full-frontal nude scene of a boy bathing outdoors. (France/Subtitles)

NAKED 1993
David Thewlis
A frontal nude scene of actor getting out of bed. (UK)

NIGHT GAMES 1967
Jorgen Lindstrom
A full-frontal nude scene of young boy. (France/Subtitles)

NIGHT TRAIN TO VENICE 1994
Unidentified
A lengthy full-frontal nude scene of a young man being dragged from his home naked by skinheads. (Germany)

1900 1977
Gerard Depardieu
Extended full-frontal nude sex scene.
Robert De Niro
Very brief frontal exposure during sex scene.
Roberto Maccanti
A full-frontal scene of two boys comparing penises.
Paolo Pavesi
A full-frontal nude scene of two boys comparing penis sizes.
Unidentified
A full-frontal long shot of a group of nude men posing for photos. (Italy/Subtitles)

NORTH OF VORTEX 1991
Unidentified
A full-frontal nude scene of black man

at the beginning of the film. (UK)
(Water Bearer)

NOT TONIGHT DARLING 1971
Vincent Ball
A full-frontal nude scene of a man
running outside.
Lance Barrett
A very brief frontal nude scene in a
bathtub.
Michael O'Malley
A full-frontal nude scene of a man
running down the street. (UK)

ODD ANGRY SHOT, THE 1979
Graeme Blundell
Extended full-frontal scene in a public
shower.
Brandon Burke
A full-frontal nude scene in a public
shower.

John Jarrett
Full-frontal shower scene.(Australia)

OVERSEAS 1991
Phillippe Galland
A very brief, frontal nude bathtub
scene. (France/Subtitles)

PARIS, FRANCE 1993
Peter Outerbridge
Several full-frontal nude scenes.
(France/Subtitles)

PASSION OF BEATRICE, THE 1988
Jean Luc Rivals
A brief, full-frontal nude scene.
(France/Subtitles)

PELLE THE CONQUERER 1988
Pelle Hvenegaard
A full-frontal nude scene of young boy

A very hunky and bushy-haired Rupert Graves (below and right) appears in a
lengthy, full-frontal nude scene getting out of bed after making love with James
Wilby, who also has a brief frontal scene in *Maurice* (1987).

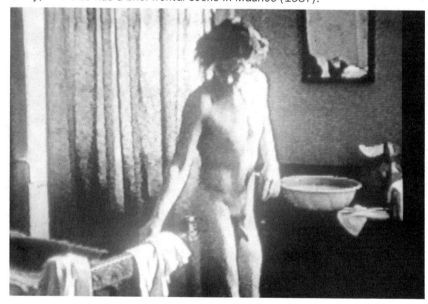

being humiliated in front of a group of people when his pants are pulled down. (Denmark-Sweden/Subtitles)

PERFORMANCE 1970
James Fox
A very brief, full-frontal nude sex scene. (UK)

PIANO, THE 1993
Harvey Keitel
A dimly-lit full-frontal sex scene with Holly Hunter.
(New Zealand)

PIXOTE 1981
Ernando Ramos da Silva
Young man appears running down a street in a full-frontal nude scene.
Unidentified Group
Full-frontal shots of a variety of nude young men in the shower.
(Brazil/Subtitles)

POLICE 1985
Jonathan Leina
A very brief, frontal, strip scene. (France/Subtitles)

PORKY'S 1981
Rod Ball, Tony Ganios, Jack Mulcahy, Cyril O'Reilly
A full-frontal nude scene of actors running out of a whorehouse.
(Canada)

PORKY'S II: THE NEXT DAY 1983
Dan Monahan
Extensive full-frontal exposure in a lengthy scene of the actor standing and running naked in a graveyard following a sexual practical joke.
Unidentified
A group of men parading around as KKK members are stripped and publicly humiliated in an extended full-frontal nude scene. (Canada)

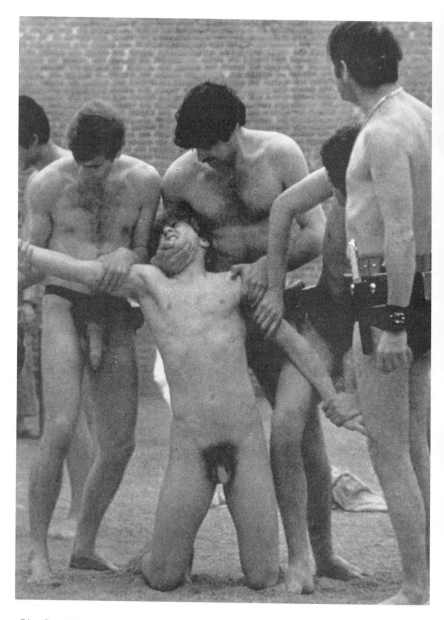

Pier Paolo Pasolini's *Salo: 120 Days Of Sodom* (1975) is the director's most controversial film and features extensive full-frontal male nudity involving numerous men of all ages.

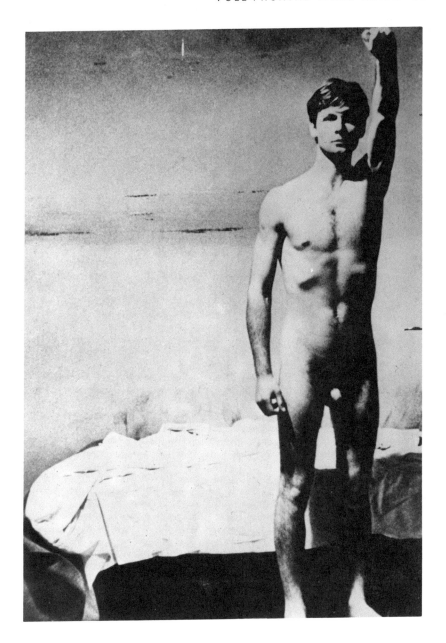

Another image from Pier Paolo Pasolini's *Salo: 120 Days Of Sodom* (1975).

Derek Jarman and Paul Humfrees' religious drama *Sebastiane* (1976) features extensive full-frontal male nudity from beginning to end.

PRETTY BOY
(a.k.a Smukke Dreng)   1992
Christian Tadrup
A full-frontal scene of a man being thrown naked out of an apartment. (Denmark/Subtitles) (IVC)

PRIEST OF LOVE   1980
Ian McKellen
Several full-frontal nude scenes. (UK)

PROSPERO'S BOOKS   1991
John Gielgud
Numerous full-frontal nude scenes of Gielgud and entire cast. (UK)

QUADROPHENIA   1979
Phil Daniels
A full-frontal bathtub scene. One of two men bathing in separate tubs in the same room.
Raymond Winston
A full-frontal nude bathtub scene. (UK)

QUARTET   1981
Jeffrey Kime
An extended full-frontal scene of a man posing as an artist's model. (UK)

QUEEN MARGOT   1994
Vincent Perez
A brief, partial-frontal nude scene while clothes are being removed. (France/Subtitles)

QUEST FOR FIRE   1981
Unidentified
A full-frontal nude scene of a man before he is eaten by cannibals. (France/Subtitles)

RASCALS, THE   1981
Unidentified
A group of boys appear in a full-frontal scene in a school shower room. (France/Subtitles)

ROAD TO SALINA   1969
Robert Walker, Jr.
A brief, frontal, skinnydipping scene. (France-Italy/Subtitles)

ROMEO AND JULIA   1981
Jean Laporte
Numerous full-frontal scenes. (Spain/Subtitles)

ROOM WITH A VIEW, A   1985
Simon Callow
An extended full-frontal nude scene of a man skinnydipping and running around a swimming hole.
Rupert Graves
A lengthy full-frontal skinnydipping scene. (UK)

RUN OF THE COUNTRY, THE   1995
Anthony Brophy
A very brief, partial-frontal nude scene of actor getting out of water after skinnydipping. (UK)

SALO: 120 DAYS OF SODOM 1975
Unidentified
Extensive full-frontal nude scenes throughout the film. (Italy/Subtitles)

SALOME'S LAST DANCE   1984
Dougie Howes
A full-frontal strip scene during a dance of the seven veils. (UK)

SALON KITTY   1975
Bekim Fehmiu
A full-frontal sex scene.
Unidentified
A frontal nude scene while exercising. (Germany/Subtitles)

SEBASTIANE 1977
Leonardo Treviglio
Extensive full-frontal nude scenes throughout the film.
Richard Warwick
Extensive full-frontal nude scenes throughout the film. (Italy/Subtitles)

SEX THIEF, THE 1973
David Warbeck
A full-frontal nude sex scene. (UK)

SHALLOW GRAVE 1994
Keith Allen
Full-frontal nude shot of a man lying dead on top of his bed. (UK)

SHIRLEY VALENTINE 1989
Tom Conti
A full-frontal, long shot, skinnydipping scene. (UK)

SIRENS 1993
Mark Gerber
A full-frontal nude scene of the actor posing for a protrait.
(Australia)

SLINGSHOT, THE 1993
Unidentified
A group of boys appear in a full-frontal nude scene while being deloused. (Sweden/Subtitles)

Jean-Hughes Anglade appears in a full-frontal nude scene in the French drama *L' Homme Blesse (The Wounded Man)*(1988).

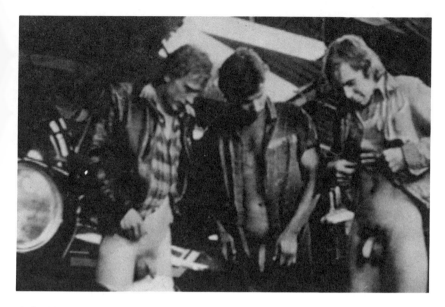

A familiar scene in coming-of-age films, three young men, Hans van Tongeren, Toon Agterberg and Maarten Spanjer, measure their penises in Paul Verhoeven's *Spetters* (1980).

SPETTERS 1980
Toon Agterberg, Maarten Spanjer, Hans Van Tongeren
Full-frontal nudity during a penis-measuring contest. (Netherlands/Subtitles)

STRAIGHT FOR THE HEART
(a.k.a A Corps Perdu) 1988
Jean-Francois Pichette
A full-frontal nude scene.
(Canada/ Subtitles)

TALL GUY, THE 1990
Neil Hamilton
A brief, difficult to see, full-frontal shot. (UK)

TAXI ZUM KLO
(a.k.a Taxi to the Toilet) 1981
Frank Ripploh

Numerous full-frontal nude, gay scenes. (Germany/Subtitles)

TEOREMA 1968
Terence Stamp
A very brief full-frontal scene of actor getting out of bed.
(Italy/Subtitles)

TINTORERA 1977
Andres Garcia
A brief frontal nude scene.
(Spain/ Subtitles)

TO FORGET VENICE 1979
David Pontremoli
A full-frontal shot during a sex scene with a woman.
(Italy/Subtitles)

Pictured above and right, Strand Releasing's black and white AIDS drama, *Via Appia* (1992), features male frontal nudity in a bathhouse.

TOM & LOLA   1992
Unidentified
A fantasy tale featuring extensive frontal nudity of a young boy and girl. (France/Subtitles) (IVC)

TO PLAY OR TO DIE   1990
Geert Hunaerts
Extended full-frontal locker room shot of this young man being teased by other students.
Unidentified Group
A group of boys appear in full-frontal scene during locker room horseplay. (Denmark/Subtitles)

TU SOLO
(a.k.a On Your Own)   1986
Luis Miguel
A full-frontal nude, moonlit, bullfight scene.
Unidentified
A full-frontal nude scene featuring a group of boys during a moonlit bull-fight. (Spain/Subtitles) (IVC)

TURKISH DELIGHT   1973
Rutger Hauer
A number of lengthy full-frontal scenes. (Denmark/Subtitles)

UN CHANT D'AMOUR   1947
Unidentified
A full-frontal nude prison scene. (France/Subtitles)

URINAL   1988
Paul Bettis
A full-frontal shower scene. (Canada/ Subtitles)

VALENTINO   1977
Rudolf Nureyev
A full-frontal nude scene of actor getting out of bed. (UK)

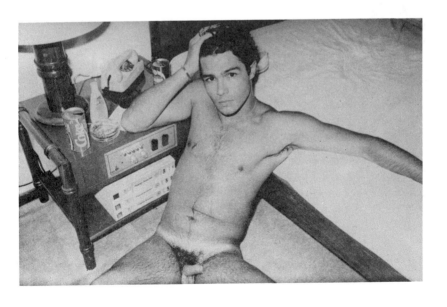

One of many full-frontal nude scenes in Pier Paolo Pasolini's *Canterbury Tales* (1971).

VIA APPIA 1991
Unidentified
A group of men appear in a full-frontal scene in a bathhouse.
(Germany/ Subtitles) (Strand)

VINCENT, FRANCOIS, PAUL AND OTHERS 1974
Frontal shot in shower after a fight.
(France/Subtitles)

WAR OF THE BUTTONS 1962
Unidentified
A group of boys appear in full-frontal scenes throughout the movie.
(France/ Subtitles)

WAR OF THE BUTTONS 1994
Gregg Fitzgerald
A dozen or more boys run naked through the woods. Includes several long shot full-frontal nude scenes.
(Ireland)

WE WERE ONE MAN 1981
(a.k.a Les Habitants De Houeilles Et Pinderes)
Piotr Stanislas
Several extensive full-frontal scenes.
(France/Subtitles)

WHAT HAVE I DONE TO DESERVE THIS? 1984
Luis Hostalot
A full-frontal shower scene before having sex with a woman. (Spain/ Subtitles)

WHEN FATHER WAS AWAY ON BUSINESS 1985
Unidentified
Young boy appears in a full-frontal scene taking a bath with a young girl and comparing body parts. Also while being circumcised. (Hungary/ Subtitles)

WIDE SARGASSO SEA 1993
Nathaniel Parker
A lengthy full-frontal scene walking across the room to his bed.
(Australia)

WILD CHILD, THE 1970
Jean-Pierre Cargol
Extensive full-frontal nude scenes of boy outdoors. (France/Subtitles)

WINDOW TO PARIS 1993
Unidentified
Three men in a nude Parisian orchestra appear in a full-frontal scene. Also includes women.
(Russia/Subtitles)

WONDERFUL, HORRIBLE LIFE OF LENI RIEFENSTAHL, THE 1993
Unidentified
Extensive full-frontal nudity in photographs of African tribe.
(Germany/ Subtitles)

WONDERLAND 1989
Emile Charles
An extended full-frontal nude scene of a man swimming in an aquarium with dolphins. (UK)

YEAR OF LIVING DANGEROUSLY, THE 1982
Unidentified
Extended full-frontal nude scene of little boy being washed by his mother.
(Australia)

YOU ARE NOT ALONE 1978
Anders Agenso, Peter Bjerg
An extended full-frontal nude scene involving two boys who fondle each other in the school showers.
(Denmark/Subtitles)

Another frontal nude shot from *The Decameron* (1970), directed by Pier Paolo Pasolini

ZED AND TWO NAUGHTS, A 1985
Brian Deacon
Extended full-frontal nude scenes.
Eric Deacon
Extended full-frontal nude scenes.
(UK)

ZERO DE CONDUITE 1932
Unidentified
A full-frontal nude scene of a group of boys in dorm room.
(France/Subtitles)

ZERO PATIENCE 1993
Unidentified
Numerous full-frontal nude scenes involving a variety of men.
(Canada/ Subtitles)

NATURIST/NUDIST VIDEOS

NATURIST/NUDIST VIDEOS

Athletes of the Sun (1993) is a popular European nudist family video featuring a group of young male athletes participating in a variety of wholesome physical activities, such as the swimming competition depicted above.

ATHLETES OF THE SUN — 1993
Dir: Jonathan Cole
Features male nature buffs of all ages at an all-male, Yugoslavian nudist retreat. (IVC)

BEACH DREAMS — 1990
(a.k.a. **Hugh Holland's Beach Dreams I**)
Dir: Hugh Holland

Youthful male naturists are featured on the nudist beaches of Mexico. (IVC)

BEACH DREAMS II — 1990
(a.k.a. **Hugh Holland's Beach Dreams II**)
Dir: Hugh Holland
More youthful male naturists on the nudist beaches of Mexico. (IVC)

1994s *FKK Mountain Men* is another popular European nudist family video featuring a group of men, young and old, on a weekend survival retreat.

Anthony Aikman's *Genesis Children* (1971) is a naturist coming-of-age classic focusing on a group of teenage nudists on a European outing.

Jonathan Cole's *Pool Buddies* (1993) captures the competitive spirit among a group of male nudists and athletes in this popular family naturist video.

BIRTHDAY BOYS 1994
Dir: John Hayman
Revolves around six young male nudists on a naturist adventure to a deserted island.
(IVC)

BODY PAINTING 1993
Dir: Jonathan Cole
An outdoor, European, naturist body painting party for the whole family.
(IVC)

BOYHOOD SCRAPBOOK 1994
(a.k.a. Slim Pfeiffer's Boyhood Scrapbook)
Dir: Slim Pfeiffer
A stills-to-video spotlighting youthful

male nudists. Features Peter Glawson and Max Adams.
(IVC)

CZECH MATES 1992
Dir: Jonathan Cole
A Czechoslovakian nudist workout featuring men of all ages.
(IVC)

DEAR CHRIS 1993
Dir: John Hayman
Features six young male nudists on a naturist outing at the Gulf of Siam.
(IVC)

FAMILY AEROBICS 1994
Dir: Jonathan Cole

European naturist video featuring in-the-buff nudist aerobics. (IVC)

FKK ALL STARS   1994
Dir: Robert Koch
A group of male nudists of all ages gather in a gymnasium for a day of nude exercise and competition. (IVC)

FKK MOUNTAIN MEN   1994
Dir: Robert Koch
A weekend retreat for boys and men at a Yugoslavian nudist lodge. (IVC)

FKK SUMMER HOLIDAY   1995
Dir: Stephan Van Houten

A day at one of Europe's most popular nudist resorts. (IVC)

FKK WATERPARK   1995
Dir: Stephan Van Houten
A weekend at Eastern Europe's most popular nudist water park. (IVC)

GENESIS CHILDREN, THE
Dir: Anthony Aikman   1971
Max Adams, Peter Glawson, Jack Good, Greg Hill
A group of young male nudists spend the summer frolicking on a secluded European beach in this coming-of-age naturist classic. (IVC)

Jonathan Cole's *Pool Buddies* (1993).

I WAS A TEENAGE NUDIST 1994
Dir: Uncredited
Seven years in the life of Bruce Nutting, voted *Natural Life* magazine's "1978 Nudist Youth of the Year." (IVC)

NAKED AFRICA 1989
Dir: David Ball
A naturist travelogue spotlighting a nude safari. Features white South Africans only. (IVC)

NAKED USA 1991
Dir: David Ball
A naturist travelogue focusing on Arizona and Nevada. (IVC)

NATURA TALENT REVIEW 1993
Dir: Jonathan Cole
A naturist talent contest featuring 85 nature buffs of all ages. (IVC)

NATURALLY NAKED 1992
Dir: Jay K. Jensen
Six male nudists get naked and explore the great outdoors. (IVC)

PETER AND THE DESERT RIDERS 1995
(a.k.a. Slim Pfeiffer's Peter and the Desert Riders)
Dir: Slim Pfeiffer
Features *Genesis Children* star Peter Glawson and co-stars Billy Marshal and Terry Stuart in a nudist adventure. (IVC)

POOL BUDDIES 1993
Dir: Jonathan Cole
European naturist video featuring nude young athletes. (IVC)

POOL PARTY, VOL 1 & 2 1992
Dir: Jonathan Cole
Outdoor naturist pool party. (IVC)

ROBBY 1968
Dir: Ralph C. Bluemke
Warren Raum, Ryp Siani
A naturist re-creation of the Robinson Crusoe tale featuring two boys stranded on an island. (IVC)

SANDY HILL 1968-71
Dir: Slim Pfeiffer
A '60s naturist nostalgia trip filmed at the old swimming hole. (IVC)

SKINNY DIPPERS 1994
Dir: Uncredited
A group of young male nudists get together for a private pool party. (IVC)

SPRING BREAK 1995
(a.k.a. Slim Pfeiffer's Spring Break)
Dir: Slim Pfeiffer
A '60s backyard swimming pool party. Features nudists Peter Glawson, Greg Hill, David Johnson, Jack Good and Sean Patrick. (IVC)

SUMMER FREEDOM 1968-71
Dir: Slim Pfeiffer
A '60s naturist nostalgia trip filmed in Corpus Christi, Texas. (IVC)

SWIM PARTY 1971
Dir: Slim Pfeiffer

Weekend Warriors (1993) is shot in Europe and features male nudists of all ages participating in an outdoor competitive Olympiad.

A playful celebration of boyhood nudism and camaraderie around the swimming pool.
(IVC)

WEEKEND WARRIORS 1993
Dir: Jonathan Cole
Fifty young male athletes gather for an outdoor nudist Olympiad.
(IVC)

WET, FIT AND NUDIST 1993
Dir: Jonathan Cole
European naturist video featuring nude men of all ages in a private nudist health club.
(IVC)

SPECIAL-INTEREST VIDEOS

SPECIAL-INTEREST VIDEOS

AMERICA'S HUNKIEST HOME VIDEOS: VOL 1-4   1995
Dir: Uncredited
Amateur home videos of hunky men stripping. (Campfire)

ART OF TOUCH I   1992
Dir: Craig Cooper
Features six handsome nude masseurs demonstrating erotic gay massage. (Alluvial)

ART OF TOUCH II   1993
Dir: Mike Esser
A 3-D guide to Taoist erotic massage featuring six sexy international models. (Alluvial)

ART OF TOUCH III: The Sports Massage   1995
Dir: Layne Derrick
Featured are four pairs of beautiful men working out in various ways, followed

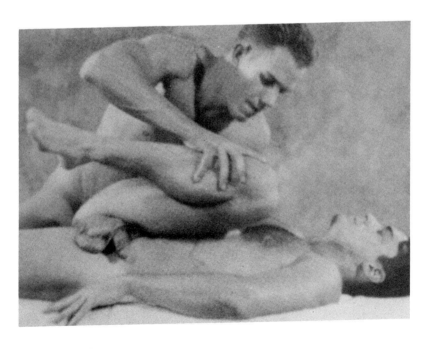

The Art Of Touch III: The Sports Massage from Alluvial-Greenwood/Cooper.

The Da Vinci Workout II: Lower Body Workout from Alluvial-Greenwood/Cooper.

by erotic, therapeutic massage.
(Alluvial)

BIGGER SPLASH, A 1974
Dir: Jack Hazan
Peter Schlesinger
Lengthy full-frontal nude scenes
throughout the film.
Unidentified
Full-frontal shots of a number of nude
young men throughout the film.

BIG SQUIRTS 1995
Dir: Edward James
An all-nude, all-male, squirt gun battle
featuring a group of college boys.
(IVC)

BLONDES & BABES
LONG HAIR BOYS 1989
(Peter Hunter's Blondes & Babes
 Long Hair Boys)
Dir: Peter Hunter
Features youthful, erotic models in
stills-to-video format. (IVC)

BLUEBOYS 1994
(Derek Powers' Blue Boys)
Dir: Derek Powers
Features youthful, erotic models in
stills-to-video format. (IVC)

BOY 1995
Dir: Uncredited
Features six uncut young men in the

A portrait of actors and models in Andy Warhol's New York studio in *Warhol,
Portrait of an Artist.*

Instincts: Erotic Choices 2 from Alluvial-Greenwood/Cooper.

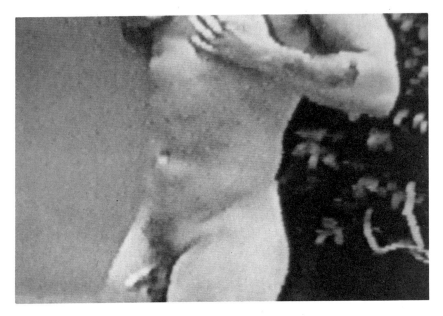

America's Hunkiest Home Videos from Campfire Video.

buff at a European spa, together and alone, in highly erotic situations. (Alluvial)

CANADIAN NUDE OIL WRESTLING VOL. 1-5   1995
Dir: Uncredited
Male nude, wrestlers compete in erotic, oiled-up competition. Each tape contains four matches. (Summers Edge)

CANADIAN NUDE PRO WRESTLING VOL. 1-3   1995
Dir: Uncredited
Hunky, male, nude wrestlers compete in realistic settings. Each tape contains four matches. (Summers Edge)

CLASSIC MALES   1994
(a.k.a. Mel Roberts' Classic Males)
Dir: Mel Roberts

Features the famed photographer's stills-to-video photo tribute to youth. (IVC)

CLASSIC MALES VOL. 2   1994
(a.k.a. Mel Roberts' Classic Males: California Dreamin')
Dir: Mel Roberts
Features Sean Patrick in a stills-to-video nostalgic tribute to youth. (IVC)

CLASSIC MALES VOL. 3   1995
(a.k.a. Mel Roberts' Classic Males 3)
Dir: Mel Roberts
Features Sean Patrick in this stills-to-video tribute to lost youth. (IVC)

COVERBOYS   1992
(a.k.a. Brad Posey's Cover Boys)
Dir: Brad Posey
Features young male models between

Scirocco from Alluvial-Greenwood/Cooper.

the ages of 18 and 21. (IVC)

COVERBOYS II　　　　　1993
(a.k.a. Brad Posey's Cover Boys II)
Dir: Brad Posey
Features more young, male models
between the ages of 18 and 21.
(IVC)

COVERBOYS III　　　　　1995
(a.k.a. Brad Posey's Cover Boys III)
Dir: Brad Posey
Features more young, male, centerfold
models between the ages of 18 and 21.
(IVC)

CRUMB　　　　　　　　1994
Dir: Terry Zwigoff
Includes numerous full-frontal draw-
ings by the infamous artist/ cartoonist
Robert Crumb.

DA VINCI BODY VOLUME I:
　　Upper Body Workout　　1992
Dir: Robby Dix
A nude, educational, exercise video
focusing on the upper body.
(Alluvial)

DA VINCI BODY VOLUME II:
　　Lower Body Workout　　1994
Dir: Kevin M. Glover
A nude, educational, exercise video
focusing on the lower body.
(Alluvial)

DA VINCI BODY VOLUME III:
　　Aerobic Workout　　　1994
Dir: Kevin M. Glover
A nude, educational, exercise video
focusing on the aerobic workout.
(Alluvial)

EROTIC CHOICES 1994
Dir: Mike Esser
An erotic, gay male, sex education
video. (Alluvial)

EURO BOY 1992
Dir: Mike Esser
Features six young men in erotic fan-
tasy situations. (IVC)

EXHIBITION 1994
Dir: Mark Lacy
A music video featuring erotic, nude
men in fantasy situations. (Alluvial)

EXOTIC BOYS 1993
Dir: Oggi
A coming-of-age sexual fantasy featur-

ing a variety of Thai young men.
(IVC)

FANTASY MEN 1992
Dir: Mike Esser
Based upon the *Euro Boy* magazine
pictorials, each video contains six hot
young men in fantasy sexual situations.
(Alluvial)

FANTASY MEN 3 & 4 1995
Dir: Mike Esser
Chris Hughes and Steve Friendly. Each
video contains six hot young men in
fantasy sexual situations, alone and
together.
(Alluvial)

In 1984, Peter Schlessinger and a number of other actors, including artist
David Hockney, appeared in several lengthy and casual, full-frontal nude scenes
in a documentary about the painter, *A Bigger Splash.*

Interludes from Alluvial-Greenwood/Cooper.

The Art Of Touch 3: The Sports Massage is the third in a series of popular, all-nude, health and exercise special-interest tapes from Alluvial-Greenwood/ Cooper Home Entertainment.

107⁰ from Alluvial-Greenwood/Cooper.

GAY MAN'S GUIDE TO
SAFER SEX 1992
Dir: Mike Esser
An erotic, safe-sex, educational video featuring a variety of men in sexual situations. (IVC)

GETTING IT RIGHT 1993
Dir: Mike Esser and Chris Hughes
An erotic, safe-sex, educational video for young men featuring a dozen men in sexual situations. (IVC)

GYMNASTIKOS:
POWER & GRACE 1993
Dir: Uncredited
Features erotic, nude, Hungarian athletes performing gymnastics with and without clothing.
(Alluvial)

HIN YIN FOR MEN 1990
Dir: Neil Tucker
A New Age video featuring ancient secrets of relaxation and self-eroticism. (IVC)

IMAGES:
SOUTH FLORIDA MEN 1995
Dir: Uncredited
A music video featuring five hot South Florida men stripping, dancing, sunning and swimming.
(Summers Edge)

INSTINCTS:
EROTIC CHOICES 2 1995
Dir: Mike Esser
A follow up to "Erotic Choices, Instincts" explores sexual techniques and alter-native positions for gay men, both

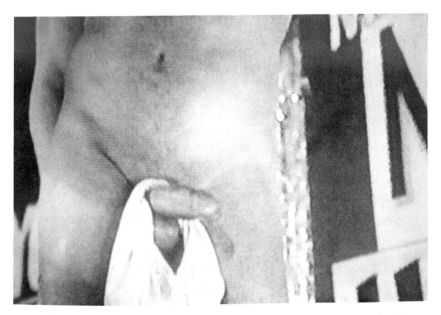

Playgirl's Mr. Nude Universe features 10 male contestants stripping, dancing and competing for the title.

individually and with partners. (Alluvial)

INTERLUDES 1995
Dir: Uncredited
This follow-up to "Fantasy Men" features eight hunky nude men in softcore voyeuristic fantasy situations. (Alluvial)

LONDON KNIGHTS 3-D 1991
Dir: Mike Esser
Ten British male strippers bare all in a variety of stylish settings and erotic fantasies.
(Alluvial)

MALEROTIC 1992
Dir: Jeremy Jensen
Features six male "works of art" in fantasy striptease situations.
(Alluvial)

MALEROTIC II 1994
Dir: Jeremy Jensen
Features a variety of male hunks in fantasy striptease situations. (Alluvial)

MAN FOR MAN VOL. 1-3 1993-95
Dir: Gordon Urquhart
An erotic video quarterly from England featuring hunky nude men in a variety of erotic fantasy situations and settings. (Water Bearer)

MEN IN LOVE 1990
Steve Warren
A brief full-frontal nude scene in this gay AIDS story. (Water Bearer)

MOVIE BUFF: THE VIDEO 1989
Dir: Uncredited
The history of male nudity in the movies. Features Jan-Michael Vincent and many others. (Campfire)

Viz from Alluvial-Greenwood/Cooper.

Trance from Alluvial-Greenwood/Cooper.

Scirocco from Alluvial-Greenwood/Cooper.

MOVIE BUFF 2:
THE SEQUEL   1989
Dir: Uncredited
The history of male nudity in the movies. Features Sylvester Stallone and many others. (Campfire)

MOVIE BUFF:
THE THREE-QUEL   1990
Dir: Uncredited
The history of male nudity in the movies. Features Jan-Michael Vincent and many others. (Campfire)

MOVIE BUFF:
THE FOUR PLAY   1991
Dir: Uncredited
The history of male nudity in the movies. Features Gregory Harrison and many others. (Campfire)

NAKED VIDEO
(SERIES) IN VOLUMES   1995
Dir: Uncredited
Erotic fantasies based on the letters sent to *Naked Magazine* by its readers. Monthly installments include much full-frontal nudity. (Summers Edge)

NOT ANGELS, BUT ANGELS   1994
Dir: Victor Grodecki
An explicit and powerful documentary look at young male hustlers in modern-day Prague. (IVC)

NUDE DUDES   1995
Dir: Joe Tiffenbach
Features a collection of nude men in natural settings. (Campfire)

NUDE MEN CAN JUMP   1995
Dir: Uncredited
Features 1995 *Playgirl* model Warren Northwood in a game of strip basketball. (IVC)

107°   1996
Dir: Uncredited
Six hunky young men come up with inventive ways to stay cool in this erotic nude fantasy. (Alluvial)

ONE FOR THE BOOKS   1992
(a.k.a. John Summers' One For The Books)
Dir: John Summers
Features five college freshmen studying for an exam. (IVC)

PINK NARCISSUS   1971
Dir: Jim Bidgood
Bobby Kendal is featured in numerous full-frontal nude scenes in this homoerotic fantasy. (IVC)

PINK ULYSSES   1971
Dir: Eric deKuyper
Jose Teunissen is featured in an homoerotic sexual fantasy. (IVC)

PLAYGIRL MAGAZINE
PRESENTS: MR. NUDE
UNIVERSE   1974
Dir: Paul Borghese
A 60-minute stage show featuring 10 hunky *Playgirl* models stripping and competing for the title. (Playgirl)

ROB LOWE'S HOME VIDEO   1989
Rob Lowe
A self-made home movie during sex.

SCIROCCO   1995
Dir: Mike Esser
A group of men share an erotic adventure in the wilderness.(Alluvial)

SENSUAL MEN   1991
Dir: N. Lee Baker and
Kurt Glowienke

A scene from *Gymnastikos: Power & Grace* from Alluvial-Greenwood/Cooper.

An erotic New Age exploration of the male body featuring a variety of hunky men. (IVC)

SEX IS ... 1993
Dir: Marc Huestis
Numerous full-frontal nude, gay sex scenes are depicted along with interviews with 15 men in this explicit sex documentary. (Water Bearer)

STRETCH: THE DA VINCI BODY SERIES VOL. 4 1996
Dir: Uncredited
Seven athletic young men guide you through nude erotic warm up routines. (Alluvial)

TRANCE 1996
Dir: Mike Esser
Six sumptuous men take a mystical erotic journey through the South African outback in an exploration of their sexual freedom. (Alluvial)

UNIQUE BOYS/THE BOYS NEXT DOOR 1990
(a.k.a. Peter Hunter's Unique Boys/ The Boys Next Door)
Dir: Peter Hunter
Features youthful erotic models in stills-to-video format. (IVC)

VIZ 1995
Dir: Tom Kurthy
Features erotic, nude men in softcore fantasy situation shot in the saunas/ baths of Budapest. Viz is Hungarian for water. (Alluvial)

WARHOL: PORTRAIT OF AN ARTIST 1989
A documentary of the infamous New York artist, filmmaker and professional celebrity. His underground films of the 1960s featured much full-frontal male nudity and made Joe Dallesandro a star.

WRESTLE 1994
Dir: Tom Kurthy
College-aged wrestlers featured in nude wrestling situations in exotic European locations. (Alluvial)

YOUNG HEARTS, BROKEN DREAMS VOL. 1-2 1995
Dir: Gerald Gordon
A gay soap opera featuring extensive full-frontal male nudity. (IVC)

Mail-Order Video Buyers' Guide

ALLUVIAL ENTERTAINMENT, INC./GREENWOOD/COOPER
8599 Santa Monica Blvd.
West Hollywood, CA 90069
800/959-9843
Call for catalog. North America's largest gay, special-interest video company. Specializes in erotic male nudity videos. "Alluvial" appears next to all of its videos listed in this guide.

AWARD FILMS INTL. & INSIDER VIDEO CLUB
PO Box 93399
Hollywood, CA 90093
800/634-2242
213/661-8330
Call for catalog. Specializes in young male, international and naturist videos. "IVC" appears next to all of its videos listed in this guide.

CAMPFIRE VIDEO
PO Box 44487
Panorama City, CA 91412-0487
No telephone
Fax: 818/893-9605
Send for catalog. Specializes in male nudity videos. "Campfire" appears next to all of its videos listed in this guide.

CINEVISTA
560 W. 43rd Street, Suite 8J
New York, NY 10036
800/341-2463
Specializes in foreign and gay-interest videos featuring male nudity.

THE PLAYBOY CATALOG
PO Box 809
Itasca, IL 60143-0809
800/423-9494
Call for catalog. Specializes in female nudity, but most videos contain male nudity as well. "Playboy" appears next to all of its videos listed in this guide.

PLAYGIRL
801 Second Avenue
New York, NY 10017
800/458-9640
Call for catalog of male nudity videos.

STRAND RELEASING
225 Santa Monica Blvd., Suite 810
Santa Monica, CA 90401
800/333-8521
Call for catalog of videos featuring male nudity. Specializes in gay-interest videos.

WATER BEARER FILMS
205 West End Ave., Suite 24H
New York, NY 10023
212/580-8185
800/551-8304
Call for catalog. Specializes in foreign and erotic male videos. "Water Bearer" appears next to all of its videos listed in this guide.

Other Sources

BARE FACTS VIDEO GUIDE
Craig Hosoda
The Bare Facts, 1995

MOVIE BUFF CHECKLIST
A History of Male Nudity
in the Movies
Marvin Jones
Campfire Productions, 1988

A PICTORAL HISTORY
OF SEX IN FILMS
Parker Tyler
Citadel, 1974

SEX IN THE MOVIES
Sam Frank
Citadel, 1986

SEX ON THE SCREEN
Gerard Lenne
St. Martin's Press, 1978

SEXUALITY IN WORLD CINEMA
James L. Limbacher
The Scarecrow Press, 1983

TOTAL EXPOSURE:
A Movie Buff's Guide
to Celebrity Nude Scenes
Jami Bernard
Citadel, 1995

THE VOYEUR'S GUIDE
TO MEN IN THE MOVIES
Mart Martin
Contemporary Books, 1994

Actor/Director Index

Title Index

One of the few Hollywood actors who appears not to be ashamed of his body, Christopher Atkins appeared naked through most of *The Blue Lagoon*.

About The Author

During a recent autograph session at Baby Jane's in West Hollywood, *Blue Lagoon* star Christopher Atkins proudly signed a full-frontal photo of himself for the author (both pictured above).

When he's not having his picture taken with Hollywood hunks, movie buff and author Steve Stewart spends his time writing about sex and nudity in the movies.

In addition to the *FULL-FRONTAL Male Nudity Video Guide*, Stewart also has written the *GAY HOLLYWOOD Film & Video Guide* (now in its second edition) and *Campy, Vampy, Trampy Movie Quotes*.

MAIL-ORDER FORM

To order by mail, photocopy
or return this page, with payment, to:
COMPANION PRESS
PO Box 2575, Laguna Hills, CA 92654

**If you would like to be added to our mailing list to receive
information about upcoming books and videos,
fill out the form below and indicate that you are over 21.
(All books and videos are discreetly mailed.)**

☐ FULL-FRONTAL—Male Nudity Video Guide $12.95

☐ SUPERSTARS—Gay Adult Video Guide $12.95

☐ The Films of KRISTEN BJORN (Available November 1996) $12.95

☐ GAY HOLLYWOOD Film & Video Guide, 2nd Edition $15.95

☐ CAMPY, VAMPY, TRAMPY Movie Quotes $9.95

(SPECIAL MAIL-ORDER OFFER: Receive *Campy, Vampy, Trampy Movie Quotes*
FREE when you purchase any two video guides at full price).

☐ Please send me the books I have checked above. I have enclosed a
check or money order (not cash) plus $1.50 PER COPY to cover postage
and handling. (Postage outside the U.S. is $5.00 PER COPY.) California
residents add 7.75% sales tax.

Name

Address

City

State   Zip

Receive Special Mail-Order Discounts and Bonus Offers